NEW DIRECTIONS FOR TEACHING AND LEARNING

Robert J. Menges, *Northwestern University*
EDITOR-IN-CHIEF

Marilla D. Svinicki, *University of Texas, Austin*
ASSOCIATE EDITOR

Changing the Way We Grade Student Performance: Classroom Assessment and the New Learning Paradigm

Rebecca S. Anderson
University of Memphis

Bruce W. Speck
University of Memphis

EDITORS

Number 74, Summer 1998

JOSSEY-BASS PUBLISHERS
San Francisco

CHANGING THE WAY WE GRADE STUDENT PERFORMANCE: CLASSROOM ASSESS-
MENT AND THE NEW LEARNING PARADIGM
Bruce W. Speck, Rebecca S. Anderson (eds.)
New Directions for Teaching and Learning, no. 74
Robert J. Menges, Editor-in-Chief
Marilla D. Svinicki, Associate Editor

ISSN 0271-0633   ISBN 0-7879-4278-2

NEW DIRECTIONS FOR TEACHING AND LEARNING is part of The Jossey-Bass
Higher and Adult Education Series and is published quarterly by Jossey-
Bass Inc., Publishers, 350 Sansome Street, San Francisco, California
94104-1342. Periodicals postage paid at San Francisco, California, and at
additional mailing offices. Postmaster: Send address changes to New
Directions for Teaching and Learning, Jossey-Bass Inc., Publishers, 350
Sansome Street, San Francisco, California 94104-1342.

New Directions for Teaching and Learning is indexed in College Student
Personnel Abstracts, Contents Pages in Education, and Current Index to
Journals in Education (ERIC).

SUBSCRIPTIONS cost $54.00 for individuals and $90.00 for institutions,
agencies, and libraries. Prices subject to change.

EDITORIAL CORRESPONDENCE should be sent to the associate editor, Marilla D. Svinicki, The Center for Teaching Effectiveness, The University of
Texas at Austin, Main 2200, Austin, TX 78712-1111.

Cover photograph by Richard Blair/Color & Light © 1990.

www.josseybass.com

ed in the United States of America on acid-free recycled paper con-
100 percent recovered waste paper, of which at least 20 percent is
umer waste.

Robert J. Menges, 1938–1998

It is a sad moment to mark the passing of our good friend and colleague, Robert Menges. We have had the privilege and pleasure of working with him on the New Directions for Teaching and Learning *series for many years. This work and his research exemplified his desire to blend research and practice in education in such a way that they nurtured one another. He had a talent for synthesizing and conceptualizing the field which few could match and which did much to move us from the field's early stirrings to its current blossoming. He was truly a gentleman and a scholar. He will be sorely missed by all.*

Marilla D. Svinicki
Associate Editor
New Directions for Teaching and Learning

FROM THE SERIES EDITORS

About This Publication. Since 1980, *New Directions for Teaching and Learning* (*NDTL*) has brought a unique blend of theory, research, and practice to leaders in postsecondary education. NDTL sourcebooks strive not only for solid substance but also for timeliness, compactness, and accessibility.

The series has four goals: to inform readers about current and future directions in teaching and learning in postsecondary education, to illuminate the context that shapes these new directions, to illustrate these new directions through examples from real settings, and to propose ways in which these new directions can be incorporated into still other settings.

This publication reflects our view that teaching deserves respect as a high form of scholarship. We believe that significant scholarship is conducted not only by researchers who report results of empirical investigations but also by practitioners who share disciplined reflections about teaching. Contributors to *NDTL* approach questions of teaching and learning as seriously as they approach substantive questions in their own disciplines, and they deal not only with pedagogical issues but also with the intellectual and social context in which these issues arise. Authors deal on the one hand with theory and research and on the other with practice, and they translate from research and theory to practice and back again.

About This Volume. Assigning grades to student work raises many dilemmas for college and university teachers. This volume helps teachers deal with these dilemmas by providing rubrics to be used as guides for scoring various kinds of student performance. More fundamentally, these chapters help teachers clarify their theories and assumptions about grading, especially useful during a time when practice is shifting from a positivist paradigm to a constructivist paradigm.

Rebecca S. Anderson, Bruce W. Speck, *Editors*
Robert J. Menges, *Editor-in-Chief*
Marilla D. Svinicki, *Associate Editor*

CONTENTS

EDITORS' NOTES   1
Rebecca S. Anderson, Bruce W. Speck

1. Why Talk About Different Ways to Grade? The Shift   5
from Traditional Assessment to Alternative Assessment
Rebecca S. Anderson
National reform efforts challenge the use of traditional assessment methods
and argue for alternative assessment practices such as performance-based
assessment, portfolio assessment, and authentic assessment.

2. Unveiling Some of the Mystery of Professional Judgment   17
in Classroom Assessment
Bruce W. Speck
Assessment of virtually any type of complex student performance has an element of subjectivity. Professors can help students realize that assessment is
not entirely mysterious by inviting students to participate in the assessment
process.

3. Grading Classroom Participation   33
John C. Bean, Dean Peterson
The quality of student classroom participation can be improved if the
instructor develops consistent and articulable standards for assessing classroom participation.

4. Designing and Grading Oral Communication Assignments   41
Brooke L. Quigley
Professors can help ease some of students' anxiety about oral presentations
by explaining to students how to prepare for oral presentations, by providing clearly articulated grading criteria, and by analyzing oral presentations
in class to explain how grading criteria are applied.

5. Designing and Grading Written Assignments   51
Eric H. Hobson
The assessment of students' writing begins with the development of the
writing assignment and the criteria that will be used to assess the final
product.

6. Grading Cooperative Projects   59
Karl A. Smith
Professors can help ensure the success of collaborative projects by preparing students to work effectively in a group. This includes using diagnostic,
formative, and summative assessment.

7. Evaluating Technology-Based Processes and Products   69
Gary R. Morrison, Steven M. Ross
Since students' technology process and products are intertwined, both can
be assessed using these techniques.

8. Portfolios: Purposeful Collections of Student Work   79
Joan A. Mullin
For many professors, portfolios are flexible enough to serve their own purposes as well as the purposes of the curriculum. Portfolios also meet the current call for authentic assessment of students' skills and performance.

9. Grading Inquiry Projects   89
Beverly Busching
Rubric-based assessment, an effective tool for grading inquiry projects,
entails students using multiple investigative methods to formulate and pursue questions of personal interest.

10. Grading Student Performance in Real-World Settings   97
Patricia A. Scanlon, Michael P. Ford
Using a variety of sources of information collected over time in the professional context by the field agency supervisor, the instructor, and the student
ensures a more informed professional judgment than traditional tests and
score sheets.

INDEX   107

EDITORS' NOTES

"Why did I get this grade on my paper?" Have you ever had a student ask you that question? Were you able to give the student a satisfactory answer—one that the student understood and felt was "fair"?

When students ask questions about grading, they are often asking about the grading process: What criteria did a professor use to derive a particular grade? What rating scale was used? Was the student informed about criteria while completing a particular task? To what extent did the professor control for the inevitable subjectivity that attends grading?

Purpose of This Volume

The purpose of this book is to provide a theoretical background for understanding issues related to grading students' performance and to give concrete examples of how to grade students' performance. We focus on performance rather than learning because learning is an abstract concept that is difficult to define, but performance is concrete and can be measured. Indeed, the best way to infer learning is by measuring changes in students' performance. Both theoretical background and concrete examples of how to measure students' performance are needed because many educators are in transition, moving from a positivist paradigm to a constructivist one. Whereas the positivist paradigm relies predominantly on lecture, passive student learning, and objective multiple-choice tests, the constructivist paradigm encourages active student learning, collaborative projects, and the use of a variety of assessment measures. Educators need to understand the rationale for the paradigm shift and be able to justify classroom practices that link pedagogy and assessment. Thus, this book provides theoretical justification for alternative assessment measures and provides examples of how those assessment measures are currently being explored in classrooms.

Although grading has traditionally been associated with summative evaluation, this volume seeks to integrate summative and formative evaluations as they relate to the learning process. This volume articulates the relationship between product and process in learning as that relationship relates to grading. For example, a teacher might assign letter grades to students' rough drafts and then average those grades to arrive at a summative evaluation. Or a teacher might require students to write journal entries for each chapter of a required text and periodically provide a grade with feedback on each set of journal entries. At the end of the semester, the teacher would give a final grade based on the quality of the final journal entries. Thus, the periodic grades would serve as formative evaluation that leads up to the final grade, which serves as summative evaluation.

NEW DIRECTIONS FOR TEACHING AND LEARNING, no. 74, Summer 1998 © Jossey-Bass Publishers

We get to the crux of the grading issue by dealing with dissonances. For instance, one dissonance is that most professors who subscribe to a constructivist paradigm see grading as a violation of that paradigm. How can a teacher help students improve their performance and then grade them? Isn't the teacher confusing the roles of coach and judge? Because we reject the positivist approach to grading—we assume that professors cannot be objective—the tension among process, product, and grade is pronounced. Another dissonance lies in terminology. Many who have written about grading often use words like *clearly, thoroughly, adequately, carefully, appropriately, accurately,* and *exceptionally* to evaluate students' performance. However, such terms are highly susceptible to interpretation. What is the connection between the terminology we use to grade and the actual act of grading? Can professors develop less abstract terminology that will convey their expectations at the outset of the learning process? Is the terminological problem a sign of a deeper issue, namely, the difficulty of specifying quality?

Overview of the Book

The two introductory chapters on theory set the stage for the following eight chapters that provide models for grading particular types of students' performance. The eight practice chapters, although written by authors from various disciplines, are interdisciplinary in their application. Each practice chapter introduces an assessment measure, provides a rationale for using it, explains how to use the assessment measure (including developing criteria, integrating peer and self-assessments, and assigning grades), discusses its advantages and disadvantages, and suggests implications for its further use. In providing examples of students' performance, authors used the types of assignments often used in constructivist classrooms. What makes the examples so meaningful is that each author has used the assessment measure he or she discusses, thus providing insight into its value and its difficulties. Many of the authors introduce rubrics, scoring scales that clearly delineate criteria and corresponding rating values to evaluate students' performance.

As a whole, this volume offers a bounty of theoretical and practical wisdom about classroom grading, but it does not claim to have solved all the knotty problems associated with grading. For instance, the accusation that grading is subjective—and unnecessarily so—is addressed in theory, but not entirely resolved in practice. In fact, a subjective element of grading may be a sine qua non that cannot be completely explained or eliminated. The chapters outline a variety of methods to implement constructivist theory in the classroom. We in no way claim that all the answers to questions about grading students' classroom performance are treated thoroughly and definitively in the following chapters. Rather, this volume provides rich examples of the potential for implementing constructivist theory in individual classrooms throughout the curriculum.

Overview of the Chapters

In Chapter One, "Why Talk About Different Ways to Grade?: The Shift from Traditional Assessment to Alternative Assessment," Rebecca S. Anderson outlines assumptions that differentiate the positivist from the constructivist approach to grading. As she points out, a theoretical approach to grading goes hand-in-hand with assumptions about how students learn. Thus, a positivist approach to grading is based on the assumption that students are passive learners. A constructivist approach assumes that students should be active learners, partners with professors in the learning and assessment enterprise.

In Chapter Two, "Unveiling Some of the Mystery of Professional Judgment in Classroom Assessment," Bruce W. Speck acknowledges the inevitable subjectivity of grading, what he calls mystery. However, professors can help students understand the need for some mystery in professional judgment by explaining many aspects of the grading process that are not mysterious.

In Chapter Three, "Grading Classroom Participation," John C. Bean and Dean Peterson tackle the problem of how to provide students with guidelines for assessing their participation, instead of using such participation as a fudge factor in determining a final grade. As do authors in several other chapters, Bean and Peterson provide rubrics that serve as models for stating grading criteria.

In Chapter Four, "Designing and Grading Oral Communication Assignments," Brooke L. Quigley explains the relationship between how a professor teaches and helps students perform and how she or he evaluates students' performance. Although Quigley focuses on oral communication assignments, her position that the design and grading of assignments are inextricably linked is shared by other authors in this volume.

In Chapter Five, "Designing and Grading Written Assignments," Eric H. Hobson provides a model for evaluating writing, beginning with the fundamental act of determining whether a professor's writing assignment provides students with adequate details about how to complete the assignment successfully. Hobson echoes Quigley's conviction that grading begins with the way an assignment is framed. This chapter walks us through a writing assignment that professors have revised to help students perform effectively.

In Chapter Six, "Grading Cooperative Projects," Karl A. Smith deals with the difficulties of grading collaborative projects. Like Hobson and Quigley, he notes how important it is for the professor to ensure that group projects are carefully explained and monitored so that students have explicit instructions about what is required and by whom.

In Chapter Seven, "Evaluating Technology-Based Processes and Products," Gary R. Morrison and Steven M. Ross explain how they evaluated students' use of technology and the products students produced via technology. Since the way technology is used is intimately associated with the products that technology yields, Morrison and Ross give helpful advice on how to think about assessing both process and products.

In Chapter Eight, "Portfolios: Purposeful Collections of Student Work," Joan A. Mullin explains how valuable portfolios can be in assessing students' performance, particularly because portfolios give students the opportunity to show a range of their performance, not just a snapshot. In addition, when used according to constructivist principles, portfolios involve students in making choices about what should be included in a portfolio and how the portfolio should be assessed. Students are further involved when portfolios include their self-assessments.

In Chapter Nine, "Grading Inquiry Projects," Beverly Busching notes the necessity of using a flexible system of assessment to evaluate student projects that differ greatly from each other because students have chosen their own topics and approaches. Busching agrees with other authors in this volume that rubrics can be extremely effective in assessing student performance, and she provides an example of a rubric she has used successfully.

In Chapter Ten, "Grading Student Performance in Real-World Settings," Patricia A. Scanlon and Michael P. Ford explain the importance of grading field experiences using a variety of assessment practices. To bring us full circle, they note the impracticality (if not impossibility) of using a positivist approach to grading field experiences by employing tests and score sheets that can be scanned to arrive at a grade. Thus, they endorse a multifarious approach to assessment that accords with a constructivist perspective.

Conclusion

Much work still needs to be done before professors across the disciplines embrace alternative assessments based on a constructivist model. We hope this volume will encourage professors who have not investigated the merits of alternative assessments to take some assessment risks and try out one or more of the practices the authors of this volume advocate. For professors who have engaged in alternative assessment, we hope they will find some insight in this volume that will enable them to hone their assessment practices. For all professors, we hope professional assessment practices will provide students with the advice and help they need to perform at the highest level possible.

Rebecca S. Anderson
Bruce W. Speck
Editors

REBECCA S. ANDERSON is codirector of the Memphis Urban Writing Institute and assistant professor at the University of Memphis.

BRUCE W. SPECK is professor of English and acting director of the Center for Academic Excellence at the University of Memphis.

*A national movement is calling for a shift from traditional assessment
to alternative assessment practices. This chapter compares the
philosophical beliefs and theoretical assumptions of traditional
assessment with those of alternative assessment and discusses the
classroom implications of shifting to an alternative assessment
paradigm.*

Why Talk About Different Ways to Grade? The Shift from Traditional Assessment to Alternative Assessment

Rebecca S. Anderson

How should students be assessed and graded? This is an age-old question, res-
onating with tensions and anxiety for both instructors and students. Yet it is
an important question, because experience and research tell us that assessment
impacts what is taught and learned in classrooms. Students spend a great deal
of time reviewing information that is assessed on tests, and instructors spend
a great deal of time teaching to the test (Crooks, 1988; Marino, Pickering, and
McTighe, 1993; Shephard, 1989, 1990).

   Currently, national reform efforts challenge the use of traditional assessment methods such as objective tests. Advocates of assessment reform argue
for alternative assessment practices such as performance-based assessment,
portfolio assessment, and authentic assessment (Belanoff and Dickson, 1991;
Darling-Hammond, 1994; Kane and Mitchell, 1996; Shulman, 1988; Tellez,
1996; Wiggins, 1989; Wilson, 1995; Witte and Flach, 1994). The purpose of
this chapter is to (1) discuss the need to shift from traditional assessment to
alternative assessment practices in higher education, (2) compare the philosophical beliefs and theoretical assumptions of traditional and alternative
assessment, and (3) discuss the implications of shifting from traditional assessment to an alternative assessment paradigm.

The Need to Shift from Traditional Assessment to Alternative Assessment

The current movement calling for a shift from traditional assessment to alternative assessment practices (Gomez, Graue, and Block, 1991; McLaughlin and

NEW DIRECTIONS FOR TEACHING AND LEARNING, no. 74, Summer 1998 © Jossey-Bass Publishers

Vogt, 1996; Perrone, 1991) involves a reconceptualization of how learning occurs. Specifically, this reconceptualization focuses on (1) the overuse of lecture as a primary teaching method and objective tests as a primary assessment measure, (2) the increasingly diverse student population in higher education classrooms, and (3) constructivist learning theory.

Overuse of Lecture and Objective Tests.   Assessment has traditionally been viewed as a means of verifying student learning (Bintz, 1991), and it occurs after learning has already taken place: "Traditionally, evaluation has been seen as an outside force that is imposed upon the curriculum generally and the learner specifically. It has been externally imposed because of several assumptions—that the questions which drive the curriculum must be supplied by outside recognized experts, that the vast majority of what is to be learned is already known, digested, and organized, and that there are acknowledged correct responses to the curricular questions which are to be asked" (Short and Burke, 1991, p. 60).

These assumptions are firmly grounded in the belief that "anything that exists at all exists in some quantity, and anything that exists in some quantity is capable of being measured" (Michaels and Karnes, 1950, p. 2). This assumption remains true today, according to Glasson and Lalik (1993) who argue that assessment has been profoundly influenced by a "Cartesian," or "positivist," epistemology that assumes one can achieve objectivity and consequently uncover "truths" about the real world. The goals of the curriculum are to teach students these "truths" by employing a transmission model of instruction and in turn to assess whether students have learned these "truths."

Traditionally, lecture has been the transmission technique most widely used in higher education. Because lecturing focuses on memorization and promotes passive learning, it is not unusual for students to daydream or not pay attention in lecture classrooms. This is evidenced by research that indicates students retain 70 percent of the information during the first ten minutes of a lecture, but only 20 percent of the last 10 minutes (McKeachie, 1994).

In lecture classrooms, evaluation of student learning is generally based on objective tests. Because lectures consist of factual information, objective tests may indeed be the most appropriate way to assess this form of instruction. However, objective tests may not be appropriate if instruction is more broad-based than merely dispensing information, such as writing-across-the-curriculum endeavors, project-based instruction, or on-line dialogues that promote active student learning and higher-level thinking skills (Sternberg, 1994).

Diverse Student Population.   Another issue related to using objective tests is the changing and increasingly diverse student population in higher education classrooms. There are more minority and nontraditional students than ever before (Farr and Trumbull, 1997). It is often argued that traditional tests are culturally biased and tend to favor white, middle-class, native-English-speaking students (Gomez, Graue, and Block, 1991), so a variety of instructional and assessment strategies that address diverse learning styles are needed (Halpern, 1994).

Constructivism.   During the past few years, much has been learned about the teaching and learning processes. One of the most current psychological theories that has contributed to this knowledge is constructivism, which is grounded in the work of Piaget (1970), Bruner (1986), and Vygotsky (1978). Brooks and Brooks (1993) offer this definition of constructivism: "Drawing on a synthesis of current work in cognitive psychology, philosophy, and anthropology, [constructivism] defines knowledge as temporary, developmental, socially and culturally mediated, and thus, non-objective. Learning from this perspective is understood as a self-regulated process of resolving inner cognitive conflicts that often become apparent through concrete experience, collaborative discourse, and reflection" (p. vii).

Education from a constructivist perspective is about assisting students to learn how to obtain knowledge. Inherent in this theory "is the idea that we as human beings have no access to an objective reality since we are constructing our version of it, while at the same time transforming it and ourselves" (Fosnot, 1996, p. 23). The focus of education takes into account the cultures and contexts in which learning occurs (Moll and Greenberg, 1990; Tittle, 1991).

Brooks and Brooks (1993), outline five overarching principles of a constructivist pedagogy: "(1) posing problems of emerging relevance to learners; (2) structuring learning around 'big ideas' or primary concepts; (3) seeking and valuing students' points of view; (4) adapting curriculum to address students' suppositions; and (5) assessing student learning in the context of teaching" (p. viii). In constructivist classrooms, students learn from active participation and have opportunities to explore their own ideas through discourse, debate, and inquiry (Anderson and Piazza, 1996; Bufkin and Bryde, 1996; Davydov, 1995; Duckworth, 1987; Kroll and LaBoskey, 1996; Gruender, 1996). Instructors assume a facilitator's role and students assume responsibility for their learning (Fosnot, 1996). Behaviors and skills are not the goals of instruction; rather, the focus is on concept development, deep understanding, and construction of active learner reorganization (Brooks, 1990). Unfortunately, traditional assessment does not evaluate this form of instruction.

Differences Between Traditional and Alternative Assessment

Although constructivism is not a theory about grading, it has implications for instructors taking a nontraditional approach to assessment (Dixon-Krauss, 1996; Steffe and Gale, 1995; Winsor, Carr, Curtis, and Odle, 1995). Constructivism supports alternative assessment practices that are at odds with traditional instruction and assessment. This section takes a closer look at these differences.

Philosophical Beliefs and Theoretical Assumptions of Traditional Assessment.   Traditional assessment is based on an interrelated set of philosophical beliefs and theoretical assumptions (Bintz, 1991). These are further outlined and compared with the philosophical beliefs and theoretical assumptions of alternative assessment in Figure 1.1. The beliefs and assumptions of traditional assessment are as follows:

Assumes Knowledge has Universal Meaning.   One assumption of traditional assessment is that knowledge has a single consensual meaning (Berlak, 1992). It is possible for everyone to reach a consensus about meaning because knowledge has "the same meaning for all individuals everywhere" (Berlak, 1992, p. 13).

Treats Learning as a Passive Process.   In traditional assessment, the metaphor of "empty vessel" is often used to talk about learners. Students are treated as if they do not possess prior knowledge about a topic. The instructor's role is "to 'fill' the students by making deposits of information which the instructor considers to constitute true knowledge" (Freire, 1990, p. 63). The focus is on learning about something rather than learning how to do something. This passive process involves students (novices) memorizing the knowledge dispensed by the text or instructor (expert).

Separates Process from Product.   Generally in traditional assessment, students' final products are evaluated based on some sort of test (Bertrand, 1993). The final outcomes of students' efforts are assumed to be representative of their learning. The how and why of student learning is not taken into consideration.

Focuses on Mastering Discrete, Isolated Bits of Information.   These bits of information basically represent lower-level thinking skills (Engel, 1994; Herman, Aschbacher, and Winters, 1992), believed to exist in a hierarchical form. Students are expected to master and demonstrate specific skills at one level before moving on to the next.

Assumes the Purpose of Assessment is to Document Learning.   Typically, traditional assessment is used only to monitor students' learning. Under this model, students who "know" are separated by those who "do not know." In other words, traditional assessment creates a system that classifies and ranks students (Berlak, 1992).

Believes That Cognitive Abilities Are Separated from Affective and Conative Abilities.   The focus of traditional assessment is primarily on cognitive abilities. The values and interests that students have about the activity being undertaken are not considered to be connected to their competence in carrying out the task (Raven, 1992). Little, if any, attention is given to students' disposition to use the skills and strategies taught or their ability to apply them (Herman, Aschbacher, and Winters, 1992).

Views Assessment as Objective, Value-Free, and Neutral.   Traditional assessment assumes that facts and values are distinct and separable entities that can be measured objectively (Berlak, 1992). Decisions about what to teach and test are not considered to be value-laden.

Embraces a Hierarchical Model of Power and Control.   In traditional assessment, generally the instructor alone has the power to make decisions about what is learned and how it is assessed (Heron, 1988; Sessions, 1995). Students do not participate in making decisions about what is important for them to learn or in determining how well they are learning.

Figure 1.1. Comparison of Philosophical Beliefs and Theoretical Assumptions of Traditional and Alternative Assessment

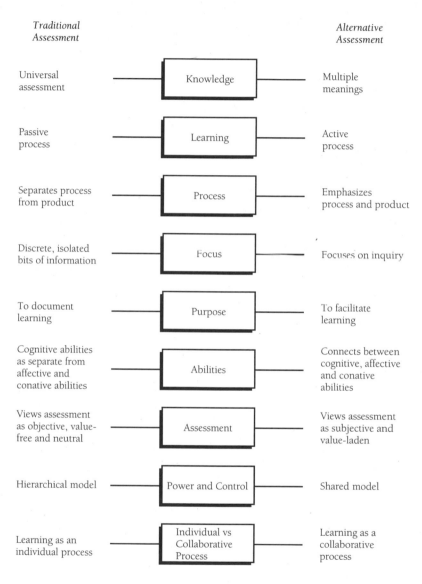

Traditional Assessment

Alternative Assessment

Traditional Assessment		Alternative Assessment
Universal assessment	Knowledge	Multiple meanings
Passive process	Learning	Active process
Separates process from product	Process	Emphasizes process and product
Discrete, isolated bits of information	Focus	Focuses on inquiry
To document learning	Purpose	To facilitate learning
Cognitive abilities as separate from affective and conative abilities	Abilities	Connects between cognitive, affective and conative abilities
Views assessment as objective, value-free and neutral	Assessment	Views assessment as subjective and value-laden
Hierarchical model	Power and Control	Shared model
Learning as an individual process	Individual vs Collaborative Process	Learning as a collaborative process

Perceives Learning as an Individual Enterprise.   Traditional assessment focuses on an individual student's performance. Students are generally expected to accomplish tasks without the assistance of others, and if they get help they are cheating. Students often work against one another in a competitive manner. "In competitive contexts, learners do not consider their own performance, and they concern themselves less with the process than with the outcome" (Johnston, 1992, p. 37).

Philosophical Beliefs and Theoretical Assumptions of Alternative Assessment.   The underlying assumptions of traditional assessment are now being challenged by advocates of alternative assessment practices. Alternative assessment is based on an entirely different set of philosophical beliefs and theoretical assumptions than traditional assessment (Bintz, 1991), as outlined in Figure 1.1. Alternative assessment has the following beliefs and assumptions:

Assumes Knowledge has Multiple Meanings.   One assumption of alternative assessment is that knowledge has "multiple realities with accompanying multiple meanings" (Roderick, 1991, p. 3). It is impossible for everyone to reach a consensus about meaning because each individual brings his or her own diverse interpretation to an ever-changing situation.

Treats Learning as an Active Process.   "Learning is a natural, integral, and ubiquitous part of living" (Bintz, 1991, p. 309). It is not something that is given to someone else. Rather, students actively search for new meanings to transform their present understanding (Greene, 1988). In other words, learning entails "producing, rather than reproducing knowledge" (Newmann and Archbald, 1992, p. 72).

Emphasizes Process and Product.   In alternative assessment practices, the process is valued as well as the product. What, how, and why students learn is taken into consideration (Hutchings, 1993; Johnston, 1992).

Focuses on Inquiry.   The focus of alternative assessment is on developing real-world problem-solving skills that will lead people to observe, think, question, and test their ideas (Herman, Aschbacher, and Winters, 1992).

Assumes the Purpose of Assessment is to Facilitate Learning.   The purpose of alternative assessment is to enhance students' learning (Johnston, 1989; Short and Burke, 1991; Wolf, 1990). When students receive feedback about their learning, they gain new direction and are able to progress in their learning. Clearly, the purpose of assessment is not to sort or classify the students.

Recognizes a Connection Between Cognitive, Affective, and Conative Abilities. When students care about the activity they are engaged in, they are more likely to invest their time and effort in it, and, as a result, they learn more from it. An assumption of alternative assessment is that "it is meaningless to attempt to assess a person's abilities except in relation to their valued goals" (Raven, 1992, p. 89).

Views Assessment as Subjective and Value-Laden.   Advocates of alternative assessment practices believe that decisions about what to teach and assess are subjective and value-laden (Bintz and Harste, 1994). "Indeed, value systems not only influence decisions about what assessment questions get answered, but also about what assessment questions get asked in the first place" (Bintz, 1991, p. 309).

Embraces a Shared Model of Power and Control.   An assumption of alternative assessment is that instructors should share the power with students to make decisions about what they learn and to determine how well they are learning. Alternative assessment embraces a democratic decision-making process (Heron, 1988).

Perceives Learning as a Collaborative Process.   In contexts that use alternative assessment practices, students and instructors are co-learners, freely expressing and testing their ideas together. In this social milieu, collaborative learning is valued, and instructors and students "are intellectually responsible to each other for creating a substantive curriculum in the classroom" (Bintz, 1991, p. 311). Advocates of the social constructivist theory of learning view assessment as part of the curriculum; they believe assessment should be guided by the same principles that guide our work in developing curriculum (Johnston, 1992; Short and Burke, 1991).

Implications of a Constructivist Assessment Paradigm

One of the major implications of embracing a constructivist assessment paradigm is that instructors' and students' roles differ from those under traditional assessment practices. In constructivist classrooms, students often have a choice about which tasks they complete and which tasks are evaluated. Furthermore, students often participate in the decision-making process of establishing the criteria to be used in the evaluation process. They establish rubrics for rating the criteria, and they engage in peer and self-evaluation. Self-evaluations guide students in making decisions about what they know and what they need to learn, which in turn influences which tasks they complete next. When instructors encourage students to become more actively engaged in the evaluation process, they relinquish complete control, embracing a more democratic stance. Yet at the same time, shifting from traditional assessment practices to a constructivist, alternative assessment paradigm raises a number of issues related to (1) instructional strategies, (2) formative and summative evaluation, (3) rubrics, and (4) instructor, peer, and self-evaluation.

Instructional Strategies.   Instructors need to critique the instructional strategies they use and the tasks they require. If lecture continues to dominate, and if students are expected to listen, read, and memorize factual information, then alternative assessment practices are not needed. Instead, a variety of tasks are needed that promote active learning, such as small group work, various writing assignments, and inquiry projects. To use such tasks, instructors need to modify in-class and out-of-class tasks. For instance, in-class small group tasks might be accomplished by students working with a partner who is sitting next to them. Out-of-class tasks that are generally completed individually can become small-group projects. Naturally, such tasks are challenging to implement in large classes taught in lecture-style auditoriums.

Formative and Summative Evaluation.   Both formative and summative evaluation procedures should be included in the assessment process. Students benefit from receiving and giving feedback on their work before the final product is completed. If students are afforded opportunities to reflect on the work they have accomplished, they can become informed about how to revise their work. Thus, some class time should be allocated for students to engage in the revision process.

Rubrics.   Students need to participate in developing the criteria and creating the rubric that is used to grade their work. This does not mean that the instructor's voice is not important. In fact, instructors should formulate tentative criteria before negotiating with students so the instructors can make suggestions in case students are slow to identify criteria. By formulating criteria before negotiating with students, instructors can feel confident that their expectations will be addressed during the grading process.

Timing is critical when developing rubrics because students often do not have the background knowledge to know what a task entails. Thus, it is difficult for them to identify criteria by which to judge a task. Providing examples that students in former classes have completed is helpful in this situation. Also, providing a rubric that a former class developed and simply modifying it can also speed up the process.

When developing rubrics, one procedure that I use is called the *four-by-four method:*

1. In small groups, students identify four characteristics of good quality in the task they are completing. (For example, the task might be a piece of writing, a classroom presentation, a double-entry journal, or a group project.)
2. Each group writes four characteristics on the chalkboard or overhead.
3. One reporter from each group discusses one characteristic from the four characteristics, perhaps the one the group discussed the most or had the greatest passion about. As the facilitator, instructors can help identify similarities and differences between the groups' criteria.
4. After each group has shared its criteria, the instructor asks the entire class to reach consensus about four criteria to be used when grading the task.
5. In small groups, students write four descriptors with a corresponding score for each of the four criteria. The scores range from 1 to 4, with 4 being the highest score.
6. After each group has shared its criteria, the class reaches group consensus.

Developing rubrics with students is time consuming. It requires class time and often creates tension for instructors because the time used to develop rubrics takes away from the amount of time used to cover course content. Instructors must decide whether their teaching focus is on helping students store knowledge or on helping students learn how to learn (Manus, 1996). Dykstra (1996), a physicist professor who holds a constructivist view, described the dilemma this way: "I could not deliver lectures and have the [students] do verification labs covering all the major topics in physics in one semester. This 'take a drink from a fire hose' approach would not do anything to induce them to challenge their notions about topics in physics, the nature of scientific knowledge, or themselves as future instructors of science to children" (p. 201). I have also found that when the teaching focus is on helping students learn how to learn, and students participate in the development of rubrics, they are clearer about what is expected of them. As a result, they learn more from the tasks.

Instructor, Peer, and Self-Evaluation.   A balance is needed between instructor, peer, and self-evaluation. Critical examination of self and others is encouraged and viewed as an important aspect of the learning process. No longer do instructors have to assume the sole responsibility of determining the students' grades. Instead, students can gain multiple perspectives on their work by engaging in peer and self-evaluation. However, this is often a new process for instructors and students. Initially, feelings of uncertainty and insecurity may abound. Students need to feel free to take risks and feel safe to make mistakes without being penalized. In addition, some students may question whether they are doing work that the instructor should be doing. I have found that generally, by the end of the semester, students are comfortable with the assessment process and appreciate the opportunity to be involved in it.

Conclusion

Moving away from traditional assessment procedures toward alternative assessments is a major theoretical change, and change takes time. It is important for instructors to move slowly and communicate to students the goals and rationale behind their alternative assessment practices. In moving toward alternative assessment, instructors should listen to students, negotiate with them, and ask for their feedback. This enables instructors to gain insight into what is working and what is not working during the transition from traditional to alternative assessment.

Embracing a constructivist, alternative assessment paradigm does not answer the question, "How should students be graded?" It is not a solution to the grading dilemma. An alternative assessment paradigm does, however, contribute greatly to formative evaluation. It connects teaching, learning, and assessment. It is a teaching tool that promotes students' learning and is a significant and powerful tool that assists instructors in being fair, thoughtful, and creative when assessing students' work.

References

Anderson, D. S., and Piazza, J. A. "Changing Beliefs: Teaching and Learning Mathematics in Constructivist Preservice Classrooms." *Action in Teacher Education,* 1996, *18* (2), 51–62.
Belanoff, P., and Dickson, M. (eds.) *Portfolios: Process and Product.* Portsmouth, N.H.: Heinemann, 1991.

Berlak, H. "The Need for a New Science of Assessment." In H. Berlak and others (eds.), *Toward a New Science of Educational Testing and Assessment.* Albany: State University of New York, 1992.

Bertrand, J. E. "Student Assessment and Evaluation." In B. Harp (ed.), *Assessment and Evaluation in Whole Language Programs.* Norwood, Mass.: Christopher-Gordon 1993.

Bintz, W. P. "'Staying Connected': Exploring New functions for Assessment." *Contemporary Education,* 1991, *62* (4), 307–312.

Bintz, W. P., and Harste, J. "Where Are We Going with Alternative Assessment? And Is It Really Worth Our Time? *Contemporary Education,* 1994, *66* (1), 7–12.

Brooks, J. G. "Instructors and Students: Constructivist Forging New Connections." *Educational Leadership,* 1990, *47* (5), 68–71.

Brooks, J. G., and Brooks, M. G. *In Search of Understanding: The Case for Constructivist Classrooms.* Alexandria, Va.: ASCD, 1993.

Bruner, J. *Actual Minds, Possible Worlds.* Cambridge, Mass.: Harvard University Press, 1986.

Bufkin, L. J., and Bryde, S. "Implementing a Constructivist Approach in Higher Education with Early Childhood Educators." *Journal of Early Childhood Instructor Education,* 1996, *17* (2), 58–65.

Crooks, T. J. "The Impact of Classroom Evaluation Practices on Students." *Review of Educational Research,* 1988, *58* (4), 438–481.

Darling-Hammond, L. "Setting Standards for Students: The Case for Authentic Assessment." *The Educational Forum,* 1994, *59* (1), 14–21.

Davydov, V. V. The Influence of L. S. Vygotsky on Education Theory, Research, and Practice." *Educational Researcher,* 1995, *24* (3), 12–21.

Dixon-Krauss, L. *Vygotsky in the Classroom: Mediated Literacy Instruction and Assessment.* New York: Longman, 1996.

Duckworth, E. *The Having of Wonderful Ideas.* New York: Instructors College Press, 1987.

Dykstra, D. I., Jr. Teaching Introductory Physics to College Students." In C. T. Fosnot (ed.), *Constructivism: Theory, Perspectives, and Practice.* New York: Teachers College Press, 1996.

Engel, B. S. "Portfolio Assessment and the New Paradigm: New Instruments and New Places." *The Educational Forum,* 1994, *59,* 22–27.

Farr, B. P., and Trumbull, E. *Assessment Alternatives for Diverse Classrooms.* Norwood, Mass.: Christopher-Gordon, 1997.

Fosnot, C. W. "Constructivism: A Psychological Theory of Learning." In C. W. Fosnot (ed.), *Constructivism: Theory, Perspectives, and Practices.* New York: Teachers College Press, 1996.

Freire, P. *Pedagogy of the Oppressed.* New York: Continuum, 1990.

Glasson, G. E., and Lalik, R. V. "Reinterpreting the Learning Cycle from a Social Constructivist Perspective: A Qualitative Study of Instructors' Beliefs and Practices. *Journal of Research in Science Teaching,* 1993, *30* (2), 187–207.

Gomez, M. L., Graue, M. E., and Block, M. N. "Reassessing Portfolio Assessment: Rhetoric and Reality." *Language Arts,* 1991, *68,* 620–628.

Greene, M. *The Dialectic of Freedom.* New York: Teachers College Press, 1988.

Gruender, C. D. Constructivism and Learning: A Philosophical Appraisal." *Educational Technology,* 1996, *36* (3), 21–29.

Halpern, D. *Changing College Classrooms: New Teaching and Learning Strategies for an Increasingly Complex World.* San Francisco: Jossey-Bass, 1994.

Herman, J. L., Aschbacher, P. R., and Winters, L. *A Practical Guide to Alternative Assessment.* Alexandria, Va: Association for Supervision and Curriculum Development, 1992.

Heron, J. "Assessment Revisited." In D. Boud (ed.), *Developing Student Autonomy in Learning.* (2nd ed.) New York: Nichols, 1988.

Hutchings, P. "Principles of Good Practice for Assessing Student Learning." *Assessment Update,* 1993, *5* (1), 6–7.

Johnston, P. H. "Constructive Evaluation and the Improvement of Teaching and Learning." *Instructors College Record,* 1989, *90* (4), 509–528.

Johnston, P. H. *Constructive Evaluation of Literate Activity.* White Plains, N.Y.: Longman, 1992.

Kane, M. B., and Mitchell, R. (eds.) *Implementing Performance Assessment: Promises, Problems, and Challenges.* N.J.: Lawrence Erlbaum, 1996.

Kroll, L. R., and LaBoskey, V. K. "Practicing What We Preach: Constructivism in a Teacher Education Program." *Action in Teacher Education,* 1996, *18* (2), 63–72.

Manus, A. L. "Procedural versus Constructivist Education: A Lesson from History." *The Educational Forum,* 1996, *60* (4), 312–316.

Marino, R. P., Pickering P., and McTighe, J. *Assessing Student Outcomes.* Alexandria, Va.: Association for Supervision and Curriculum Development, 1993.

McKeachie, W. *Teaching Tips: Strategies, Research and Theory for College and University Instructors.* Lexington, Miss.: D. C. Heath, 1994.

McLaughlin, M., and Vogt, M. *Portfolios in Teacher Education.* Newark, Del.: International Reading Association, 1996.

Michaels, W., and Karnes, M. R. *Measuring Educational Achievement.* New York: McGraw-Hill, 1950.

Moll, L. C., and Greenberg, J. B. "Creating Zones of Possibilities: Combining Social Contexts for Instruction." In L. C. Moll (ed.), *Vygotsky and Education: Instructional Implications of Sociohistorical Psychology.* Cambridge, N.Y.: Cambridge University Press, 1990.

Newmann, F. M., and Archbald, D. A. "The Nature of Authentic Academic Achievement." In H. Berlak and others (eds.), *Toward a New Science of Educational Testing and Assessment.* Albany: State University of New York, 1992.

Perrone, V. (ed.) *Expanding Student Assessment.* Alexandria, Va.: Association for Supervision and Curriculum Development, 1991.

Piaget, J. *The Science of Education and the Psychology of the Child.* New York: Basic Books, 1970.

Raven, J. "A Model of Competence, Motivation, and Behavior, and a Paradigm for Assessment." In H. Berlak and others (eds.), *Toward a New Science of Educational Testing and Assessment.* Albany: State University of New York, 1992.

Roderick, J. A. (ed.) *Context-Responsive Approaches to Assessing Children's Language.* Urbana, Ill.: National Conference on Research in English, 1991.

Sessions, R. "Education is a Gift, Not a Commodity." Paper presented at the National Conference of the Community Colleges Humanities Association, Washington, D.C., November 1995.

Shepard, L. A. "Why We Need Better Assessments." *Educational Leadership,* 1989, *46* (7), 4–9.

Shepard, L. A. "Inflated Test Score Gains: Is the Problem Old Norms or Teaching the Test?" *Educational Measurement: Issues and Practice,* 1990, *4,* 15–22.

Short, K. G., and Burke, C. *Creating Curriculum: Instructors and Students as a Community of Learners.* Portsmouth, N.H.: Heinemann, 1991.

Shulman, L. S. "A Union of Insufficiencies: Strategies for Teacher Assessment in a Period of Educational Reform." *Educational Leadership,* 1988, *46* (3), 36–41.

Steffe, L. P., and Gale, J. *Constructivism in Education.* Hillsdale, N.J.: Lawrence Erlbaum, 1995.

Sternberg, R. J. "Diversifying Instruction and Assessment." *The Educational Forum,* 1994, *59* (1), 47–52.

Tellez, K. "Authentic Assessment." In J. Sikula (ed.), *Handbook of Research on Teacher Education.* (2nd ed.) New York: Simon & Schuster Macmillan, 1996.

Tittle, C. K. "Changing Models of Student and Instructor Assessment." *Educational Psychologist,* 1991, *26* (2), 157–165.

Vygotsky, L. S. *Mind in Society: The Development of Higher Psychological Processes.* Cambridge, Mass.: Harvard University Press, 1978.

Wiggins, G. "A True Test: Toward More Authentic and Equitable Assessment." *Phi Delta Kappan,* 1989, *71,* 703–713.

Wilson, S. M. "Performance-Based Assessment of Teachers." In S. W. Soled (ed.), *Assessment, Testing, and Evaluation in Teacher Education.* Norwood, N.J.: Ablex, 1995.

Winsor, J. L., Carr, K. S., Curtis, D. B., and Odle, C. "Assessment as a Unifier of Teaching and Research." Paper presented at the annual meeting of the Central States Communication Association, Indianapolis, Ind., April 1995.

Witte, S. P., and Flach, J. "Notes Toward an Assessment of Advanced Ability to Communicate." *Assessing Writing, 1* (2), 207–246.

Wolf, D. P. "Assessment as an Episode of Learning." Paper presented at the Conference of Constructive Response, Princeton, N.J., November 1990.

REBECCA S. ANDERSON is codirector of the Memphis Urban Writing Institute and assistant professor at the University of Memphis.

When students understand and are involved in the grading process, professors unveil some of the mystery of professional judgment and validate the need for professional judgment.

Unveiling Some of the Mystery of Professional Judgment in Classroom Assessment

Bruce W. Speck

Professional judgment is central to grading students' various performances, but professional judgment often seems "mysterious" or unpredictable, not only to the laity but even to professionals themselves. Because it is based on interpretation of a highly complex object—such as a piece of writing, an oral presentation, a long-term project that results in a physical model, a portfolio of work, or a musical performance—professional judgment can appear to be unreliable, both in terms of intrarater and interrater reliability. For instance, studies have shown that graders do not agree among themselves about the grade a paper should receive (Diederich, 1974; Dulek and Shelby, 1981). In addition, graders are not consistent when they evaluate the same paper a second time (Branthwaite, Trueman, and Berrisford, 1981; Edwards, 1982). Indeed, the literature on peer review of journal manuscripts (for example, Fiske and Fogg, 1990), book manuscripts (for example, Ross, 1979), and grant applications (for example, McCullough, 1989) confirms the "mystery" of professional judgment concerning writing. The problem of professional judgment is not restricted to judgments about written texts. It extends, for instance, to judgments physicians render, as Eddy (1996) illustrates. In fact, I surmise that judgments in virtually any profession have a mysteriousness about them because they cannot overcome the problem of subjectivity.

The catch in "the problem of subjectivity" is that a professional judgment of a complex task—such as Olympic figure skating—requires *personal* professional judgment that is by nature subjective to some extent. Therefore, to criticize subjectivity in toto is to undercut professional judgment itself, to recommend that professional judgment be replaced by a test of reliability that disallows for professional *judgment*. Even when managers evaluate employees at the end of a rating period using standards, the managers must use judgment in applying those standards to each employee's performance. Applying standards to individual performance requires a judgment based on the interpretation of various sorts of data, and the type and length of a manager's training and experience will no doubt affect the way he or she interprets data. Such is the nature and mystery of professional judgment, in assessing students' performance and in assessing a wide variety of performances in virtually every profession.

To confirm the necessary presence of subjectivity and the concomitant mystery is not to deny the need to unveil that mystery to some extent. In fact, I argue that professors should probe that mystery with their students so that students recognize the necessity of subjectivity in professional judgment (Belanoff, 1993). Such probing begins by recognizing that grading is (or should be) part and parcel of the entire teaching enterprise. Grading is not something that is done merely at the end of an assignment or a course; rather, grading should be woven into the classroom tapestry throughout the course.

One difficulty of advocating that grading not be limited to the end of an assignment or course is that the term *grading* is most often associated with summative evaluation, generally a literal grade or score that purports to sum up a judgment about the value of a student's work and efforts. To suggest that grading is not necessarily summative seems to fly in the face of the common use of the term *grading*. While grading certainly can be summative, I submit that the term *grading* also refers to a formative process that includes establishing standards and discussing how to apply those standards. To divorce the grading process from the actual grade is to promote the false concept that the process used to derive a grade is a complete mystery, unable to be investigated. My complaint about such a divorce is that the goal of the process then becomes a grade, rather than improved student performance. Thus, grades often appear to be the ultimate value—to students, professors, administrators, and employers. Little wonder that so much depends on grade point averages. Scholarships, admittance to graduate schools, job opportunities, parental approval, peer approval, and even self-esteem are based, often in large part, on grades (Pollio and Humphreys, 1988). Perhaps part of the reason that the process of grading lies in the shadow of the result of that process (the grade itself) is that the process is shrouded in the mystery of professional judgment.

My purpose in this chapter is to investigate that mystery by examining (1) the language of grading, (2) the relationship between evaluation and academic standards, and (3) ethical issues related to grading. My investigation is based on the premise that professional judgment is central to the grading process, but professional judgment is only one source of legitimate grading. I argue that classroom grading entails a much larger role for the teacher, a role that includes explaining some of the mystery of grading to students. The purpose of explaining some of the mystery of grading is to help students realize that grading includes, but is not limited to, the professor's subjective professional judgment of students' efforts.

The Language of Grading

One of the mysteries associated with grading is the language used to talk about it. The mystery of that language can be traced to two sources: Diverse uses of the language and theoretical positions that inform uses of the language.

Diverse Uses of the Language of Grading. *Marking, assessing, evaluating,* and *grading* are often used interchangeably in literature about classroom grading. Unfortunately, all four terms are imprecise and lead to confusion. For instance, although *marking* would seem to be the most precise term of the lot—after all, marking is putting marks on a student's paper—the term is used to mean grading in the sense of evaluating (Kline, 1976; Land and Evans, 1987). In fact, the term *marking* is often part of a cluster of terms that includes responding, providing feedback, commenting, and engaging in dialogue. Thus, as Hillocks (1982) points out in discussing teacher comments, marking has "at least two functions—to justify a particular grade assigned and to advise students on ways to improve their writing" (p. 80). However, even if marking meant nothing more than putting marks on a student's paper, we might still ask various questions about those marks. What is the purpose of the marks? Are there good and bad ways to mark a student's paper? What's the difference, if any, between marking a student's paper and responding to it?

The lack of uniformity in the use of the grading language certainly helps promote some of the mystery of grading. If the very people who write about grading—mostly educators—don't use the same terms or don't use the same terms in the same ways to describe what they are doing, students can be expected to respond in one of two ways. First, students could assume a particular definition of grading and use that definition to interpret what professors say when they talk about grading. For instance, students could translate any discussion about grading to mean "the grade." When students take this approach to grading, they may assume that grading is mysterious and unable to be unveiled, so they want to know about outcomes, not the basis for those outcomes, the process used to derive "the grade."

For example, although answers to certain circumscribed questions about, say, the mechanics of driving a vehicle—such as how to start a car, how to put it in gear, how to read a speedometer, and how to stop the car—are prerequisites to driving a car, they are not sufficient when drivers are required to make judgments about, say, whether to proceed through a yellow light. Successful student performance generally assumes some level of such knowledge, but when students confuse the acquisition of knowledge that can be assessed using tests requiring correct answers with the application of that knowledge to complex performance tasks requiring professional judgment, they fail to appreciate the need for professional judgment that invariably is subjective in some measure. If they fail to appreciate the need for professional judgment and are not taught how to participate in professional judgments, students do not learn how to use professional judgment effectively. They can easily believe that making judgments is a responsibility of those with certain status, as though status alone confers the ability to make professional judgments.

Grading by mimicking professional judgment, by the way, seems to me to be the predominant method professors use in assessing student performance. They take as a model a professor (or a composite of professors) they studied under, and they grade students' performance according to the mystery they admired but did not unveil.

In pointing out the misunderstanding students might develop, I am not criticizing students. Rather, I am criticizing educators, including professors. When students make the mistake of equating the grading of answers to objective tests with the grading of student performance that requires the application of objective test knowledge, they are demonstrating that educators have not done enough to unveil the mystery of grading student performance. Thus, the professor's role is not only to render professional judgments but to help students understand as much as possible how those judgments were obtained.

Confusion in professors' use of the language of grading could lead students to another response. Instead of assuming that grading is defined in a particular way, students could attempt to determine what a particular professor means when he or she talks about grading. The type of questions students generally ask, however, to unveil how professors define grading often deal with discrete or surface issues, such as the length of an assignment, not with substantive issues, such as how quality is defined after issues related to discrete or surface issues are dealt with. In this second approach, students may be concerned about the mystery of grading, but they ask for measurable information to decipher that mystery. Again, students seek to quantify the unquantifiable, the mysterious. However, students need to learn how to ask questions that will help them unveil *some* of the mystery of grading, although not all of it can be unveiled.

Professors can help students understand the basis of grading by explaining what they do, and by asking appropriate questions and suggesting some answers. For instance, professors can ask students, What are the characteristics of an excellent oral presentation? Do we need to give more evaluative weight to some characteristics than to others? How do we determine how much weight to give any particular characteristic? The professor can suggest answers to these questions in the spirit of mentoring the class. That is, the professor can explain that his or her answers are based on past performances the professor has seen, and he or she can include many examples of common pitfalls, some examples of high quality, and other data that students may not have access to. The professor also can ask students to draw on their knowledge by encouraging them to think about similar performances they have witnessed outside the classroom. For example, if students are doing oral presentations, they should think of other oral presentations they have heard: sermons, political speeches, graduation speeches, keynote addresses, and so forth. In asking students to connect student oral presentations with oral presentations beyond the classroom, the professor can help students see the relationship between student and professional performance. Thus, students might realize that what they are doing is related to what they will do after they leave school and that evaluative criteria apply both to classroom and professional performances. In providing questions and suggesting answers, the professor establishes a framework for unveiling some of the mystery of grading, thus helping students to understand that when the process of grading is contextualized, the grade is less mysterious and more meaningful.

Theoretical Positions and the Language of Grading. Confusion about the language of grading also can be attributed to two different theoretical views, or paradigms, of grading. As Chapter One of this volume elaborated, one theoretical view, positivism, promotes an objective view of grading. The positivist teacher focuses on right and wrong answers. For instance, a positivist exercise in grammar would ask students to identify parts of speech. Identifying parts of speech, however, can have greater educational value when used in the service of answering more complex questions about language. Thus, the professor who believes that students should learn grammar to identify errors also should explain to students that all grammatical errors are not equal because errors have a social dimension (Harris, 1997). When a person uses the word *ain't*, the error is not one of ineffective communication; native speakers of English know that *ain't* means will not. The error is social; educated people tend to look down on a person who uses *ain't* without showing in some way that such usage is nonstandard. *Ain't* is not wrong because it does not communicate negation. It is "wrong" in certain social contexts because it reveals low social awareness of language conventions associated with high social status. Unfortunately, a positivist approach to grading language use stresses right and wrong answers in absolute terms ("No educated person would use *ain't*") and, therefore, reduces the process of grading to an evaluation of rote memorization skills students use to identify error. Memorizing usage rules and applying them without recourse to the ebb and flow of social convention can become an end in itself. Thus, professors (and students) sometimes mistakenly assume that the ability to identify usage "errors" enables a person to write effectively, even when research has shown that grammar-based writing instruction may actually impair students' ability to write (Hillocks, 1986, p. 214).

Another theoretical view, constructivism, does not hold that all knowledge is objective, something stable and countable that students can receive and commit to memory. Constructivists believe that knowledge is socially constructed, that people make meaning through interacting with their environment (Witte and Flach, 1994). Therefore, rote learning or memorization of accepted concepts is not learning in the true sense of the word. For constructivists, learning is based on highly personal interaction with ideas and physical artifacts.

This does not mean that no standards are used to measure student performance. For instance, a constructivist could use a rubric—one that the students either help develop at the beginning of a project or receive copies of so that they will know what the grading standards are at the outset of a project. A constructivist professor also might ask students to evaluate themselves so that the professor can use those evaluations to derive a grade for an assignment or a course. How the professor uses those evaluations still contains mystery, because constructivism cannot fully account for the mystery of professional judgment. However, constructivism does provide good reasons why professors and students should develop standards together and come to some agreement about what standards should be applied to evaluate students' performance (Murphy, 1994).

My purpose here is not to give a full-blown treatment of the contrast between positivism and constructivism, but to show that each theoretical position is based on assumptions about the nature of grading. Thus, a positivist uses the term *grading* in a different way than a constructivist does. When positivists use any of the cluster of terms associated with grading, they are basing their arguments on classical testing theory, which focuses on summative evaluation. When constructivists use any of these same terms, they are basing their arguments on the positions espoused by such theorists as Bakhtin, Polyani, and Vygotsky, who promote collaborative learning. In other words, positivists believe in standards based on "objective" measures, that is, statistically verified judgments, and constructivists believe in standards based on "subjective" measures, that is, teacher judgment. For the positivist, grading means using a scientific process, generally based on statistical data, to ensure that the product, a student's grade, is valid and reliable. For the constructivist, grading means using a collaborative approach that is open-ended to ensure that students participate in the development of grading standards and the administration of grades. As even a cursory review of the theoretical underpinnings of positivism and constructivism shows, different uses of grading terms by proponents of different theoretical positions adds to the mystery of defining the cluster of terms associated with "grading."

Formative and Summative Assessment.   One way to make at least two distinctions about the meaning or role of grading is to use the terms *formative* and *summative assessment*. For instance, Calfee and Freedman (1996) make the following distinction between the two terms: "For formative evaluation, standards gauge learning and instruction conjointly; for summative evaluation, standards gauge the level of accomplishment" (p. 22). While these terms have some value in distinguishing between the process and product of grading, ultimately, the terms formative and summative assessment obscure the fact that together they constitute a whole piece of cloth. To suggest that formative assessment is not a prelude to summative assessment or that summative assessment cannot be used within the grading process in a series of plateaus between formative assessments that lead to the final summation is to promote a false dichotomy. As Calfee and Freedman (1996) go on to say, "Although these two sets of standards need to mesh, they are very different in character" (p. 22). How they mesh is the crucial question. Professors may give little careful thought to formative assessment and, in practice, often limit themselves to summative assessment, but such an approach serves to further veil the mystery of grading.

For the remainder of this chapter, I will use the terms *formative* and *summative assessment* because they help differentiate between the process of grading and the product of grading—the grade. However, I use those terms realizing that the relationship between process—formative assessment—and product—summative assessment—is not clearly understood. In fact, the tension between formative and summative assessment leads to an investigation of the relationship between assessment and academic standards.

The Relationship Between Assessment and Academic Standards

At the heart of the assessment debate is tension in the relationship between assessment and academic standards. That tension can be illustrated by considering a major purpose of classroom assessment: certification. Did the student learn enough in one course to be "certified," and thus probably successful in another course? Did the student learn enough to earn credit for a class? For many students, the pressing question is, Will I earn enough credits to graduate and be awarded the certification represented by a degree? Questions about certification are tenacious, bottom-line questions bound up with issues of accountability, educational funding, professorial training, and a host of social and political issues.

Questions about certification are quite complex. For instance, if Weeks (1978) is correct when he says that grades have different meanings for different audiences, then we might ask whether grades really can certify competency. If grades have an inherent ambiguity, an inherent mystery, then what exactly is certified by a grade or by grades in the aggregate? According to Agnew (1995), decontextualized grades are meaningless: "The fact that low grades, high grades, *any* grades in isolation reveal nothing about institutional standards, quality of teaching, or student skills seems to have been overlooked by administrators, politicians, department heads, and (even) professors eager to latch onto some quantifiable 'proof' that students are being held to the 'rigorous grading standards' that Cole [another writer] recommends. In isolation, grades are meaningless" (p. 94).

Weeks' and Agnew's reasoning is difficult to refute. In fact, grades, while perhaps able to point out high academic achievement, appear unable to provide important data about human behavior, as the case of the Unabomber demonstrates (Jackson, 1997).

To address the problem of mystery that both Weeks and Agnew pinpoint, professors have used two tactics. They either advocate the abolition of grades or promote local standards. Those who want to solve the mystery of meaninglessness by abolishing grades say that summative assessment is an enemy of teaching and learning (McDonald, 1973). One problem with this proposal is that it assumes an antithesis without proving it. Just because grades appear to lack generalizable meaning as they are currently used does not mean that grades are always meaningless. The proposal to abolish grades also appears to disregard the certification aspect of grading. If grades are abolished, what should take their place so that institutions of higher education can certify their graduates in some way? However, the most significant problem with this abolitionist proposal is that it does not address ways professors can unveil the mystery of formative assessment. To abolish grades is only to do away with a common form of summative assessment; such abolition does not answer questions about formative assessment. Professors would be hard pressed to defend the abolition of their responsibilities to facilitate and participate in formative assessment.

Others want to resolve the tension between grading and academic standards by establishing local standards. That is, they advocate having professors in a particular locale, whether a university or a state-wide system of higher education, develop standards in consultation with each other. This proposal has the merit of providing a mechanism for professors to unveil some of the mystery of grading by talking with each other about standards and articulating standards that they agree on. Those standards then can be explained to students.

The most ambitious and publicized attempt to develop local standards and unveil some of the mystery of assessment is portfolio assessment. One advantage of using portfolios in the classroom is that, when administered in certain ways, they can unveil some of the mystery of assessment by allowing students to participate in the assessment process (for example, see Gottlieb, 1995; Knight, 1992; Metzger and Bryant, 1993). Belanoff (1991) goes so far as to say that the two types of valid judgments, personal and communal, can be integrated most effectively through portfolio assessment. Cooper and Brown (1992) say that portfolios "can be a valuable source for summative evaluation. . . . and have potential for formative assessment" (p. 45).

Nevertheless, portfolios are problematic (Hamp-Lyons and Condon, 1993; Nystrand, Cohen, and Dowling, 1993). Valencia (1991) states, "Unless we are committed to spending sufficient time to study carefully the potential advantages and problems of portfolios, they are destined to fail" (p, 44). White (1992), in looking to the future of portfolios as an assessment tool, notes, "the advantages of portfolios, great as they are, seem at present to be balanced by a series of problems that may or may not be manageable" (p. 72). If portfolios are to become an effective assessment tool, White says, "we will have to learn how to handle this new assessment device with care, fairness, economy, and responsibility" (p. 73). In other words, the jury is still out on portfolio assessment as a valid method for developing local standards. (See Chapter Eight in this volume for a fuller discussion of how to use portfolio evaluation in the classroom.)

One difficulty with developing local standards at the university level is professorial autonomy. Professors may not want to develop assessment standards, either formative or summative, in a community setting. Sometimes resistance to locally developed community standards is defended on the basis of academic freedom, the belief that the professor is in charge of the classroom and nobody has the right to tell the professor how to teach his or her subject. While such a definition of academic freedom can be debated, the attitude behind that definition is often so firmly entrenched that the real issue is professional pride and insecurity. As Sloan (1977) says, "I had always felt an inexplicable reluctance to ask colleagues for permission to examine themes they had marked. I would've sooner requested permission to scrutinize their wallets and purses" (p. 370).

Dealing effectively with professional pride and insecurity is beyond the purview of this chapter, but in as much as pride and insecurity hinder attempts to unveil some of the mystery of grading, they need to be addressed. For Bullock (1991), the need to address such issues is urgent. He notes that student assessment "cannot rest on a single reading by an isolated teacher"; rather, "without shared values, writing assessment is doomed to subjectivity" (p. 192). Whether subjectivity in and of itself dooms assessment and whether shared values is the remedy for such subjectivity are debatable. Nevertheless, Bullock's general concern about subjectivity could be extended to any assessment of student performance.

In short, the debate about the relationship between grading and academic standards is really a debate about how to define learning and measure it, and about who should do that defining and measuring. One tricky aspect of this debate is that professors are seen as the experts on learning, but the certification most professors receive to teach—the doctorate—has been limited historically to one subject area. Instruction in pedagogy, including how to assess students' learning, has been disdained, even though many who earn doctorates become university professors who are required to teach as part of their job.

The insufficiency of graduate training to meet the professors' pedagogical responsibilities is an impetus for the writing-across the-curriculum programs. When are professors of engineering, business, or psychology taught how to use writing effectively in their classes? Perhaps they learn to use writing effectively in their classrooms through faculty development activities, after they receive the Ph.D. and begin to teach. But such faculty development activities have occurred only recently, spurred on by the writing-across-the-curriculum movement. Indeed, the Ph.D. in English, for instance, does not guarantee that a professor can teach writing effectively. Traditionally, professors of English literature have been trained to write literary criticism, a specialized kind of writing, but they are expected to teach introductory writing courses. Such courses call for a variety of written forms, many of which English literature professors have not studied and are not qualified to teach. The assumption that a Ph.D. prepares anyone to teach is ill founded. Rarely do doctoral programs include instruction on how to construct effective examinations, including the preparation of valid and reliable prompts; how to give effective feedback—both formative and summative—to students on their performance; and how to help demystify the grading process. Clearly, one of the most pressing needs in higher education is the linking of training in teaching effectiveness with expertise in an academic discipline. Much of the mystery of classroom assessment should be unveiled systematically during professors' graduate education, including pressing ethical issues.

Ethical Issues Related to Classroom Assessment

The central ethical issue in classroom assessment is the dilemma of the professor balancing two conflicting roles: coach and judge (Belanger, 1985; Ede, 1980). How can the professor, in good faith, assign tasks to students, help the students fulfill those tasks (even by clarifying the requirements for a particular assignment, not to mention providing substantive information through such means as lecturing), and then evaluate students' performance? Isn't the professor in some measure evaluating his or her own performance when evaluating students' performance? Doesn't this put the professor in an ethical bind?

The resounding answer to the last question, given throughout the literature on classroom grading, is Yes. In fact, the inherent subjectivity of professional judgment and professors' lack of meta-analysis of classroom assessment that would lead to a theory of grading (Speck and Jones, 1998) complicate ethical issues. When, indeed, professional judgment and lack of meta-analysis are implicated in the coach-judge dilemma, ethical concerns about classroom assessment intensify. Commonly, these concerns are expressed in terms of fairness. Is it fair for professors to be both coach and judge when they don't seem to be able to defend their dual role outside of an appeal to professional status?

Questions of fairness related to the coach-judge dilemma are really questions about the relationship between formative (coaching) assessment and summative (judging) assessment. That one person can be both trainer and rater seems prima facie to be unethical. Thus, professors have proposed a variety of techniques to deal with the coach-judge dilemma, including exchange grading (Tritt, 1983), team grading (Grogan and Daiker, 1989), external evaluators (Sawyer 1975, 1976), and teacher-student grading (Barbour, 1992). The goal of these solutions to the judge-coach dilemma is to somehow separate the coaching function from the judging function either by involving students in the process so that they have input into the grade or by dispersing the authority for grading to others, either students, other professors, or other professionals.

Whether the solutions help unveil some of the mystery of grading depends in part on (1) the continuity between the professor's role as a coach in explaining the entire assessment process and functioning as a coach effectively, (2) the judges' use of explicit and public criteria in assessing students' performances, and (3) the use of an appeal system to allow for checks and balances of judges' verdicts.

Ethical questions about classroom assessment, however, are not concentrated on the coach-judge nexus. The coaching process itself raises ethical questions. Are professors good trainers/coaches? Are they, in ethical terms, fulfilling their responsibilities as professional coaches? Can they be trusted to provide professional judgments that are valuable, not misleading, and not in error?

Those questions are, of course, difficult to answer, but we can at least note that part of the answer resides in our understanding of authority in the classroom. On one hand, by virtue of his or her position, the professor has claims to authority that are not shared by the students. The professor, in most cases, has intellectual authority by virtue of academic training. However, the professor does not necessarily possess superior intellectual ability, and a professor does not have a corner on intellectual insights even in his or her area of expertise, whether that be educational theory, mechanical engineering, Kantian philosophy, or computer programming. One implication of these various professional authorities is that the classroom needs to be a community of students—including the professor—that allows each member to function successfully given the various dynamics of authorities inherent in the classroom (Speck, in press).

Literature on grading offers a variety of methods for ensuring that the dynamics of authorities are integrated into the classroom, including grading contracts (Hassencahl, 1979; Knapp, 1976) and grading rubrics (Allen, 1988). Such methods allow for student choice and participation in the assessment process. During the actual process of formative assessment—reading a student's written work, for instance, to give feedback for revision—certain ethical problems can hinder the professor from unveiling some of the mystery of assessment and thereby promote an authoritarian stance that counters the dynamics of authorities. Thus, professors can read students' writing primarily to find errors (Williams, 1981), instead of recognizing that error can be a sign of risk taking and learning (Kroll and Schafer, 1987). To counter this error-prone approach to reading, professors might consider using praise in responding to students (Daiker, 1989; Dragga, 1988; Zak, 1990) or at least modify a predominantly negative approach of error hunting by including comments that acknowledge a student's communicative successes (Reed and Burton, 1985). Professors can ensure multiple readings of students' work (whether sculptures, science projects, performances, or written texts) by building into the class structure peer evaluations (Belcher, 1990; Mittan, 1989). Professors also can help students unveil the mystery of assessment by providing a framework for student self-evaluations (Boud, 1989; MacGregor, 1993; McNamara and Deane, 1995).

When a professor does give feedback to students, that feedback should be based on the same principles the professor espoused as a coach. Unfortunately, professors don't always practice what they preach in giving feedback. As Heffernan (1983) says of writing professors' war against sentence fragments, "Though we condemn our students for writing what we call sentence fragments, our own comments to them are not even complete words: they are *word* fragments—mere letters, teacherspeak, a code that operates on what is figuratively as well as literally the mere margin of language. In this as in so many other aspects of the grading process we are indeed telling our students to do like we *say* do, not do like we *do*" (p. 3).

Professors of writing may misidentify or be unable to identify usage errors (Greenbaum and Taylor, 1981) and, because of professors' idiosyncratic concepts of language, they may indoctrinate students "with strange prescriptions" about writing "rules" (Harris, 1979). Indeed, professors of English do not necessarily agree in every case what constitutes an error (Wall and Hull, 1989). If such is the case for those who have credentials to teach English, it is not unreasonable to suggest that the same problems, particularly regarding the assessment of student writing, are common to professors throughout the disciplines.

In addition, professors should not assume that students will interpret feedback according to the professor's intention (Cohen, 1987; Newkirk, 1984; Smith, 1989), so professors should (1) demonstrate their own analytical and writing abilities by providing useful feedback, not comments such as "awkward" (Clark, 1984; Dohrer, 1991) and (2) use student-professor conferences to provide an opportunity for students to ask questions about the professor's feedback (Harris, 1986).

Professors can address ethical concerns about classroom assessment by recognizing the ethical dilemma embodied in the coach-judge role and by implementing methods of assessment that provide for student choice and involvement in the entire assessment process, formative and summative. If, however, professors do not have the necessary training to assess students' performances, then faculty development training is needed. Professors, as is the case with other professionals, have a responsibility to perform at a high level in their chosen field, teaching for professors. If, for whatever reason, professors are not able to satisfy that professional responsibility, they should acquire the skills they need to do their job. We would not expect a stock broker to invest our money, lose it, and then tell us that he or she really didn't know enough about the financial instruments and markets into which our money disappeared. Such incompetence is intolerable in financial and in educational investments. It is, in fact, intolerable in any profession.

Conclusion

Professors have a particular responsibility to help students unveil some of the mystery of professional judgment. This is true not only because professors have a professional responsibility to understand and explain educational practices (Angelo, 1990), but also because professors are inducting students into responsible assessment models that students might find useful when they become professional evaluators. In inducting students into responsible assessment, professors can use a variety of methods, many outlined in this chapter, to unveil some of the mystery of grading so that the presence of subjectivity is not seen as a cause for perceived unfair assessments.

Other than lack of training in classroom assessment, the most significant hurdle professors face in learning how to assess students' performance is professional hubris. If professors believe that the classroom is their special domain, a place where they reign with complete and uncontested authority under the aegis of academic freedom, then my proposal to unveil some of the mystery of classroom assessment likely will appear to be an assault on an academic bastion. While I certainly agree that professorial authority is necessary in the classroom, I simply point out that the focus of the classroom is not professorial authority, but learning. When professorial authority becomes a hindrance to learning, professors should be the first to raise objections. Thus, when the mystery of classroom assessment dumbfounds even the practitioners of such assessment, it is time for professors to take a hard look at the mystery and unveil much of it for themselves. Such unveiling is needed and can have a salutary effect on classroom practices.

References

Allen, J. "A Machiavellian Approach to Grading Writing Assignments." *The Technical Writing Teacher,* 1988, *15* (2), 158–160.

Agnew, E. "Rigorous Grading Does Not Raise Standards: It Only Lowers Grades." *Assessing Writing,* 1995, *2* (1), 91–103.

Angelo, T. A. "Classroom Assessment: Improving Learning Quality When It Matters Most." In M. D. Svinick (ed.), *The Changing Face of College Teaching.* San Francisco: Jossey-Bass, 1990.

Barbour, D. H. "The Best of Both Worlds: Instructor/Group Evaluation of Business Writing Assignments." *Journal of Business and Technical Communication,* 1992, *6* (4), 480–487.

Belanger, J. "Conflict Between Mentor and Judge: Being Fair and Being Helpful in Composition Evaluation." *English Quarterly,* 1985, *18* (4), 79–92.

Belanoff, P. "What Is a Grade?" In W. Bishop (ed.), *The Subject Is Writing: Essays by Teachers and Students.* Portsmouth, N.H.: Boynton/Cook, 1993.

Belanoff, P. "The Myth of Assessment." *Journal of Basic Writing,* 1991, *10* (1), 54–66.

Belcher, D. D. "Peer vs. Teacher Response in the Advanced Composition Class." *Issues in Writing,* 1990, *2* (2), 128–150.

Boud, D. "The Role of Self-Assessment in Student Grading." *Assessment and Evaluation in Higher Education,* 1989, *14* (1), 20–30.

Branthwaite, A., Trueman, M., and Berrisford, T. "Unreliability of Marking: Further Evidence of a Possible Explanation." *Education Review,* 1981, *33* (1), 41–46.

Bullock, R. "Autonomy and Community in the Evaluation of Writing." In R. Bullock and J. Trimbur (eds.), *The Politics of Writing Instructions: Postsecondary.* Portsmouth, N.H.: Heinemann, 1991.

Calfee, R. C., and Freedman, S. W. "Classroom Writing Portfolios: Old, New, Borrowed, Blue." In R. Calfee and P. Perfumo (eds.), *Writing Portfolios in the Classroom: Policy and Practice, Promise and Peril.* Mahwah, N.J.: Lawrence Erlbaum, 1996.

Clark, B. L. "Responding to Students: Ughs, Awks, and Ahas." *Improving College and University Teaching,* 1984, *32* (4), 169–172.

Cohen, A. D. "Student Processing of Feedback on their Compositions." In A. Wenden and J. Rubin (eds.), *Learner Strategies in Language Learning.* New York: Oxford University Press, 1987.

Cooper, W., and Brown, B. J. "Using Portfolios to Empower Student Writers." *English Journal,* 1992, *81* (2), 40–45.

Daiker, D. A. "Learning to Praise." In C. M. Anson (ed.), *Writing and Response: Theory, Practice, and Research.* Urbana, Ill.: NCTE, 1989.

Diederich, P. B. *Measuring Growth in English.* Urbana, Ill.: NCTE, 1974.

Dohrer, G. "Do Professors' Comments on Students' Papers Help?" *College Teaching,* 1991, *39* (2), 48–54.

Dragga, S. "The Effects of Praiseworthy Grading on Students and Teachers." *Journal of Teaching Writing,* 1988, *7* (1), 41–50.

Dulek, R., and Shelby, A. "Varying Evaluative Criteria: A Factor in Differential Grading." *The Journal of Business Communication,* 1981, *18* (2), 41–50.

Eddy, D. M. "Variations in Physician Practice: The Role of Uncertainty." In *Clinical Decision Making: From Theory to Practice.* Sudbury, Mass.: Jones and Bartlett, 1996.

Ede, L. "Audiences, Paradigms, Role Playing and Evaluation: Some Implications." *Kansas English,* 1980, 65, 8–10.

Edwards, D. "Project Marking: Some Problems and Issues." *Teaching at a Distance,* 1982, *21,* 28–34.

Fiske, D. W., and Fogg, L. "But the Reviewers Are Making Different Criticisms of My Paper!: Diversity and Uniqueness in Reviewer Comments." *American Psychologist,* 1990, *45* (5), 591–598.

Gottlieb, M. "Nurturing Student Learning Through Portfolios." *TESOL Journal,* 1995, 5 (1), 12–14.

Greenbaum, S., and Taylor, J. "The Recognition of Usage Errors by Professors of Freshman Composition." *College Composition and Communication,* 1981, *32* (2), 169–174.

Grogan, N., and Daiker, D. A. "Team-Grading in College Composition." *WPA: Writing Program Administration,* 1989, *13* (1–2), 25–33.

Hamp-Lyons, L., and Condon, W. "Questioning Assumptions About Portfolio-Based Assessment." *College Composition and Communication,* 1993, *44,* 176–190.

Harris, J. "Error." In *A Teaching Subject: Composition Since 1966.* Upper Saddle River, N.J.: Prentice Hall, 1997.

Harris, M. *Teaching One-to-One: The Writing Conference.* Urbana, Ill.: NCTE, 1986.

Harris, M. "Contradictory Perceptions of Rules for Writing." *College Composition and Communication,* 1979, *30* (2), 218–220.

Hassencahl, F. "Contract Grading in the Classroom." *Improving College and University Teaching,* 1979, 27 (1), 30–33.

Heffernan, J.A.W. "Getting the Red Out: Grading Without Degrading." Paper presented at the annual meeting of the Conference on College Composition and Communication. Detroit, Mich., March 17–19, 1983. ED 229 788.

Hillocks, G., Jr. *Research on Written Composition: New Directions for Teaching.* Urbana, Ill.: NCRE ERIC, 1986.

Hillocks, G., Jr. "Getting the Most Out of Time Spent Marking Compositions." *English Journal,* 1982, *71* (6), 80–83.

Jackson, D. S. "Man Behind the Mask." *Time,* November 17, 1997, *150* (21), 52.

Kline, C. R., Jr. "I Know You Think You Know What I Said." *College English,* 37 (7), 661–662.

Knapp, J. V. "Contract/Conference Evaluation of Freshman Composition." *College English,* 1976, 37 (7), 647–653.

Knight, P. "How I Use Portfolios in Mathematics." *Educational Leadership,* 1992, *49,* 71–72.

Kroll, B. M., and Schafer, J. C. "Error-Analysis and the Teaching of Composition." In T. Enos (ed.), *A Sourcebook for Basic Writing Teachers.* New York: Random House, 1987.

Land, R. E., Jr., and Evans, S. "What Our Students Taught Us About Paper Marking." *English Journal,* 1987, *76* (2), 113–116.

MacGregor, T. (ed.) *Student Self-Evaluation: Fostering Reflective-Learning.* San Francisco, Calif.: Jossey-Bass, 1993.

McCullough, J. "First Comprehensive Study of NSF Applicants Focuses on Their Concerns About Proposal Review." *Science, Technology, & Human Values,* 1989, *14* (1), 78–88.

McDonald, W. U., Jr. "Pass/No Pass Credit in Beginning Composition: Problems and Promise." *College Composition and Communication,* 1973, *24* (5), 409–413.

McNamara, M. J., and Deane, D. "Self-Assessment Activities: Toward Autonomy in Language Learning." *TESOL Journal,* 1995, 5 (1), 17–21.

Metzger, E., and Bryant, L. "Portfolio Assessment: Pedagogy, Power, and the Student." *Teaching English in the Two-Year College,* December 1993, 279–288.

Mittan, R. "The Peer Review Process: Harnessing Students' Communicative Power." In D. M. Johnson and D. H. Roen (eds.), *Richness in Writing: Empowering ESL Students.* New York: Longman, 1989.

Murphy, S. "Portfolios and Curriculum Reform. Patterns in Practice." *Assessing Writing,* 1994, *1* (2), 175–206.

Newkirk, N. "How Students Read Student Papers: An Exploratory Study." *Written Communication,* 1984, *1* (3), 283–305.

Nystrand, M., Cohen, A. S., and Dowling, N. M. "Addressing Reliability Problems in Portfolio Assessment of College Writing." *Educational Assessment,* 1993, *1* (1), 53–70.

Pollio, H. R., and Humphreys, W. L. "Grading Students." In J. H. McMillan (ed.), *Assessing Students' Learning.* San Francisco, Calif.: Jossey-Bass, 1988.

Reed, W. M., and Burton, J. K. "Effective and Ineffective Evaluation of Essays: Perspectives of College Freshmen." *Journal of Teaching Writing,* 1985, *4* (2), 270–283.

Ross, C. "Rejected." *New West,* 1979, *4* (4), 39–43.

Sawyer, T. M. "External Examiners: Separating Teaching from Grading." *Engineering Education,* 1976, *66* (4), 344–346.

Sawyer, T. M. "Accountability: Or Let Others Grade Your Students." *College Composition and Communication,* 1975, *26* (4), 335–340.

Sloan, G. "The Wacky World of Theme-Marking." *College Composition and Communication,* 28, 370–372.

Smith, E. "'It Doesn't Bother Me, But Sometimes It's Discouraging': Students Respond to Teachers' Written Responses." *Journal of Teaching Writing,* 1989, 8, 253–265.

Speck, B. W. "The Teacher's Role in the Pluralistic Classroom." Perspectives, in press 28 (1), 19–43.

Speck, B. W., and Jones, T. "Direction in the Grading of Writing?: What the Literature on the Grading of Writing Does and Doesn't Tell Us." In F. Zak and C. Weaver (eds.), *The Theory and Practice of Grading Writing: Problems and Possibilities.* New York: State University of New York Press, 1998.

Tritt, M. "Exchange Grading with a Workshop Approach to the Teaching of Writing." *English Quarterly,* 1983, *16* (1), 16–19.

Valencia, S. W. "Portfolios: Panacea or Pandora's Box?" In F. L. Finch (ed.), *Educational Performance Assessment.* Chicago: Riverside, 1991.

Wall, S. V., and Hull, G. A. "The Semantics of Error: What Do Teachers Know?" In C. M. Anson (ed.), *Writing and Response: Theory, Practice, and Research.* Urbana, Ill.: NCTE, 1989.

Weeks, F. W. "The Meaning of Grades." In G. H. Douglas (ed.), *The Teaching of Business Communication.* Champaign, Ill.: American Business Communication Association, 1978.

White, E. M. "Using Portfolios: Definitions, Strengths, and Weaknesses." In *Assigning, Responding, Evaluating: A Writing Teacher's Guide.* New York: St. Martin's, 1992.

Williams, J. M. "The Phenomenology of Error." *College Composition and Communication,* 1981, *32,* 152–168.

Witte, S. P., and Flach, J. "Notes Toward an Assessment of Advanced Ability to Communicate." *Assessing Writing,* 1994, *1* (2), 207–246.

Zak, F. "Exclusively Positive Responses to Students Writing." *Journal of Basic Writing,* 1990, *9* (2), 40–53.

BRUCE W. SPECK is professor of English and acting director of the Center for Academic Excellence at the University of Memphis.

Grading class participation signals students about the kind of learning and thinking an instructor values. This chapter describes three models of class participation, several models for assessment including a sample rubric, problems with assessing classroom participation, and strategies for overcoming these problems.

Grading Classroom Participation

John C. Bean, Dean Peterson

A recent study of core curriculum syllabi at Seattle University revealed that 93 percent of courses included class participation as a component of course grades. Our informal discussions with professors, however, suggest that most professors determine participation grades impressionistically, using class participation largely as a fudge factor in computing final course grades. This phenomenon helps explain why assessment and measurement scholars almost universally advise *against* grading class participation (see Davis, 1993, pp. 80, 283). According to Jacobs and Chase (1992), weighing student behaviors into a course grade "contaminate[s] the grade as a measure of achievement of the course objectives" (p. 195). Jacobs and Chase identify several reasons for not grading class participation: professors generally don't provide instruction on how to improve participation; interpretation of student behavior is difficult and subjective; participation often depends on a student's personality, thus disadvantaging shy or introverted students; record-keeping is problematic; participation scores for a given individual are hard to justify if challenged.

Despite these objections, we believe that grading class participation can send positive signals to students about the kind of learning and thinking an instructor values, such as growth in critical thinking, active learning, development of listening and speaking skills needed for career success, and the ability to join a discipline's conversation. By explaining these values to students, professors can justify the emphasis they place on class participation. Moreover, research reveals that students with a high grade orientation value only those portions of a course that are visibly graded (Marzano and others, 1988, p. 137; Janzow and Eison, 1990). When students see that their participation is being graded regularly and consistently, they adjust their study habits accordingly to be prepared for active participation.

We contend that the problem of impressionism in assessing classroom participation can be substantially alleviated through scoring rubrics analogous to holistic or analytic rubrics used in assessing writing (for example, White, 1994). In the following pages we describe three different modes of class participation and provide several models for assessment including a sample rubric. We then examine problems with assessing classroom participation and suggest strategies for overcoming them.

Modes of Classroom Participation

Before explaining how we grade class participation, we should identify briefly the various ways a participatory classroom can be structured. The most common participatory classroom uses what we might call open or whole-class discussion, wherein the instructor poses questions aimed at drawing all class members into conversation. To facilitate whole-class discussion, the instructor might request a U-shaped case classroom, move chairs into a horseshoe or circle, or otherwise adjust space so that students can address each other without passing all commentary through the instructor (Welty, 1989).

Another method, common among professors who value think-on-your-feet Socratic examination, is the "cold-calling" mode, fixed in the popular imagination by Professor Kingsfield in the 1972 film *The Paper Chase*. In cold-calling, the professor poses a question and then calls on students at random to formulate their answers. In assessing student responses, many professors take into account the difficulty level of the question posed, often using a taxonomy such as that of Bloom (1956). Whereas the open-discussion professor tends to value any kind of question or response from students, the cold-calling professor often assesses the student for quality of response during the Socratic examination.

Still another kind of participatory class employs collaborative learning, in which students work in small groups toward a consensus solution of problems designed by the instructor and then report their solutions in a plenary session. Differences among group solutions often lead to whole-class discussions during the plenary session (Johnson and Johnson, 1991; Bruffee, 1993).

In addition to these modes of class participation, some professors also count such out-of-class behaviors as email discussions on class listserves, timely completion of out-of-class journal entries, collaboration on group homework projects, or even conferences with the instructor during office hours.

Developing an Assessment Measure: A Prototype Example

In this section we'll outline a prototypical method for developing an assessment measure, in this case for a professor who combines whole-class discussion with occasional small group work. The instructor's first task is to envision what an ideal class session would look like. For example, during an ideal whole-class discussion, all students would participate, and the discussion itself would reveal dialogic inquiry characterized by empathic listening to other students' views as well as reasonably high levels of critical thinking. (For characteristics of an ideal class discussion, see Baron, 1987, pp. 230–31).

To develop an assessment measure, the prototypical instructor, near the outset of a course, negotiates with students the criteria for successful class participation. The instructor can begin by asking the class to think of times when class discussion has gone well for them: "What were the features of those discussions?" the professor can ask. "What behaviors did students exhibit? What was the professor's role versus the students' role in making good discussions happen?" As the instructor records students' responses on the chalkboard, he or she can add his or her own criteria to the list. The instructor's goal is to show how effective discussion can develop critical thinking and lead to higher levels of learning.

Once a master list of the traits and features of an ideal discussion is on the board, the instructor and students can formulate guidelines for individual behaviors (both students' and instructor's) that will help create effective discussions. From this list, an instructor can create a holistic rubric for assessing class participation (see Exhibit 3.1). Using such a rubric, the instructor can assign students points for class discussion at several different times in the term.

Additionally, the prototypical instructor can ask students to write a self-assessment of their own participation. The instructor might ask students questions such as these: (1) Where do you currently rank yourself on the scoring rubric? Why? (2) What might you do to improve the quality of your own participation? (3) What can the instructor do to help improve classroom discussions? (4) What do you like best and least about classroom discussions over the last two weeks? Such self-assessments encourage students to think reflectively about their role in class discussions and provide professors with useful data about students' perceptions of the classroom environment. When the student's self-assessment differs substantially from the instructor's, the self-evaluation can be a useful starting place for a student-professor conference. We have found, for example, that students whom we would rate as 5's or 6's on the rubric often fear that they are 4's; we occasionally find too that students with hostile or bored body language are actually enjoying discussions and are unaware of their body signals.

Finally, some professors might ask students to rank each other on the scoring rubric. These peer rankings can then be averaged and compared to the instructor's ranking to increase the reliability of the measure.

Exhibit 3.1. Holistic Rubric for Scoring Class Participation

6   A student receiving a 6 comes to class prepared;[1] contributes readily to the conversation but doesn't dominate it; makes thoughtful contributions that advance the conversation; shows interest in and respect for others' views; participates actively in small groups.

5   Comes to class prepared and makes thoughtful comments when called upon; contributes occasionally without prompting; shows interest in and respect for others' views; participates actively in small groups. A 5 score may also be appropriate to an active participant whose contributions are less developed or cogent than those of a 6 but still advance the conversation.

4   A student receiving a 4 participates in discussion, but in a problematic way. Such students may talk too much, make rambling or tangential contributions, continually interrupt the instructor with digressive questions, bluff their way when unprepared, or otherwise dominate discussions, not acknowledging cues of annoyance from instructor or students. Students in this category often profit from a conference with the instructor.

3   A student receiving a 3 comes to class prepared, but does not voluntarily contribute to discussions and gives only minimal answers when called upon. Nevertheless these students show interest in the discussion, listen attentively, and take notes. Students in this category may be shy or introverted. The instructor may choose to give such students a 5 if they participate fully in small group discussions or if they make progress in overcoming shyness as the course progresses. Sympathetic counseling of such students often helps.[2]

2–1   Students in this range often seem on the margins of the class and may have a negative effect on the participation of others. Students receiving a 2 often don't participate because they haven't read the material or done the homework. Students receiving a 1 may be actually disruptive, radiating negative energy via hostile or bored body language, or be overtly rude.

NOTE: This scoring guide assumes regular attendance; the instructor may lower participation scores for absences or tardiness.

1. Preparation can be measured by quizzes, by brief writing assignments at the start of class, by completion of out-of-class journal entries or other homework, or by evidence from direct questioning.
2. During class discussions of this rubric, we have found that students often want to reverse the 4's and the 3's. They will argue that a quiet student who actively listens deserves more points that the dominating/annoying student. Teachers may wish to follow this suggestion.

Varying the Prototype: Alternative Ways to Assess Participation

In this section, we turn from a hypothetical instructor to actual case examples of two professors whose strategies for assessing class participation vary from the preceding prototype. Our goal in this section is to emphasize the range of options that professors have for assessing participation.

Our first example of an alternative assessment strategy—based on a cold-calling approach—is used by co-author Dean Peterson in his Principles of Macroeconomics class. At the beginning of the term, Peterson announces that classroom participation will be graded and included as a part of the homework component for the computation of final grades. Students are told to expect to be called on individually to give definitions, explain relationships, or respond to articles taken from popular media sources such as the *New York Times* or *Business Week*. Peterson determines which students he will query by drawing names from a randomly shuffled deck of 3 × 5 cards, each card bearing the name of one student. Satisfactory answers are recorded on the cards as a 2 (strong answer), 1 (satisfactory answer), or 0 (unsatisfactory answer or absence). At the end of the term, Peterson uses the numbers to create a ratio, the numerator determined by the sum of the points received and the denominator by the number of questions a student was asked times 2 (the maximum points possible for each question). The resultant ratio is then multiplied by the total number of points allotted for class participation in Peterson's grading scheme for the course.

Peterson's random cold calling motivates students to become energetic readers of assigned material. Peterson channels this energy by distributing in advance lists of topics from assigned readings (terms, concepts, questions requiring critical thinking) for which students will be responsible during each day's cold calls. (Additionally, all previously discussed material is fair game for cold calls.) Peterson uses cold-calling in roughly three quarters of his class sessions. The number of questions asked and the time devoted to this technique vary considerably depending on the amount of study material distributed in advance.

A possible weakness of Peterson's card approach is that it does not take into account the difficulty level of the question asked. Professors wishing to construct a more sophisticated measure can adopt strategies suggested by Stiggins, Rubel, and Quellmalz (1986), who present a scoring chart based on Bloom's taxonomy of educational objectives. A similar grading scheme (Sanders, 1966) allows professors to measure student performance on a 1–10 point scale with the most points allotted to satisfactory answers to difficult questions.

Another approach to grading class participation, vastly different from Peterson's cold-calling method, is taken by history professor Arthur Fisher of Seattle University, who rejects holistic scales, record-keeping, and other attempts to create empirical data. In an email message to us, Fisher stated, "I believe that all grading is primarily subjective, and I tell students so on the first day. . . . What I measure, I tell them, is whether I think that they are adults with respect to the material, or if not, then what share of adult they are." In some of his history classes, Fisher bases up to half the course grade on students' ability to carry on committed and sustained discussion. Students are expected to come to class having actively grappled with the course readings, which are predominately primary sources. In his syllabus, Fisher explains that during class discussion "the authors' assumptions, objectives, forms of argument, adduced evidence, and conclusions" will all be laid bare. Along with participating in the daily classroom discussion, students are required to keep a notebook "in which they are to accumulate their jottings and reflections on the readings" (course syllabus).

On a typical day, Fisher initiates the day's discussion and then intervenes only when needed to ensure that important points are covered. At the end of the term, Fisher grades the participation *subjectively* based on his impressions of students' performance and his evaluation of the reading notebooks which he collects periodically during the course at random. By *not* creating point systems, scales, and other attempts to objectify classroom performance, Fisher assumes the role of supportive but demanding coach interested in holistic performance. Unable to accumulate points (and bicker about them), students set out simply to impress the professor that they are "adults with respect to the material." Fisher's results, based on peer observations, on student performance on papers and exams, and on student ratings, are excellent.

The strength of Fisher's approach is that the extensive weight placed on class participation, combined with Fisher's careful observation and coaching of students' behaviors, leads to high-level performance. A weakness, some might argue, is that the lack of regularly assigned points may limit students' opportunity to evaluate and improve their performance and may make the final class participation grade seem more arbitrary.

Problem Areas and Suggestions for Overcoming Them

The assessment of class participation raises knotty problems about how to distribute participation so that the most extroverted students don't dominate the discussion while others sit silently. To grade class participation fairly, the instructor needs to create an environment that gives all students an opportunity to participate. Many of these problems are solved by Peterson's cold-calling method since the opportunity to speak is distributed randomly by the shuffling of the cards. But for professors who use whole-class discussion with limited prompting from the instructor, they need other means of inviting the silent to speak and quieting the extroverts. This section offers several strategies.

Strategy 1: Create Activities in Which Participants Report on Homework Already Prepared.   Often, quiet people are more comfortable speaking in class if they can prepare ahead of time. Co-author John Bean assigns "guided journals" in which students write a one-page journal entry prior to each class in response to a question passed out in advance (Bean, 1996, pp. 107–108). A student can be called on to summarize what he or she wrote in a journal, thus reducing the anxiety of having to respond to a question extemporaneously. A related strategy is reported by Angelo and Cross (1993), who describe how a calculus instructor modified a student learning assessment technique to promote active participation in discussions (pp. 38–40).

Strategy 2: Include an Email Component for Class Participation. Another strategy is to conduct some class discussions on email. Many students who are pathologically quiet in class come to life through email. Reports of successful strategies for incorporating email in a course are becoming more common in the literature (Meacham, 1994; Bhide, 1996).

Strategy 3: Increase Wait Time.   A third method of leveling the playing field in classroom participation is to pose a question and then to enforce a minute or so of silence for students to structure their reply. Some professors ask students to write non-stop during this time to get initial ideas down on paper. After a minute or so, the instructor asks for volunteers or calls on a selected student.

Strategy 4: Use a "Card System" for Shy Students.   Professors might also consider using "comment cards" for shy students. Students who are reluctant to participate in class might be allowed to turn in 3 × 5 cards bearing their responses to questions posed during discussion.

Strategy 5: Develop Techniques for Quieting Discussion Dominators (rubric category 4 in Figure 3.1).   A number of writers have addressed the problem of the overly talkative or rambling student. McKeachie (1986, p. 37), for example, suggests that professors assign one or two students to act as "observers" with the duty of reporting to the class the extent to which participation is evenly distributed. The instructor might even assign a discussion monopolizer to be an observer for a day. (See Davis, 1993, p. 79 for a helpful summary of strategies for quieting discussion dominators).

Strategy 6: Coach Problematic Students and Reward Progress.   Professors can also invite students who are not successfully participating in class to an office conference where the instructor can speak honestly about the problem and listen to students' perspectives and concerns. Through supportive coaching, students may begin to make small steps toward progress—steps which the instructor can visibly reward.

Conclusion

Our premise in this article is that the quality of student performance during class discussions can be improved if the instructor develops consistent and articulable standards for assessing classroom participation. We suggest several options for assessing participation and believe that professors must choose the approach that best matches their course goals and pedagogical methods. In conjunction with effective writing assignments and with examinations that test at the higher levels of Bloom's taxonomy, an instructor's method for assessing classroom participation is one of a whole set of signals about the kind of thinking and learning valued in a course.

References

Angelo, T. A., and Cross, K. P. *Classroom Assessment Techniques: A Handbook for College Professors.* (2nd ed.) San Francisco: Jossey-Bass, 1993.

Baron, J. B. "Evaluating Thinking Skills in the Classroom." In J. B. Baron and R. J. Sternberg (eds.), *Teaching Thinking Skills: Theory and Practice.* New York: W. H. Freeman, 1987.

Bean, J. C. *Engaging Ideas: The Professor's Guide to Integrating Writing, Critical Thinking, and Active Learning in the Classroom.* San Francisco: Jossey-Bass, 1996.

Bhide, A. "Using Technology." *Harvard Business School Publishing Newsletter,* Fall 1996, 1–2.

Bloom, B. S. (ed.). *Taxonomy of Educational Objectives. Volume 1: Cognitive Domain*. New York: McKay, 1956.

Bruffee, K. A. *Collaborative Learning: Higher Education, Interdependence, and the Authority of Knowledge*. Baltimore: Johns Hopkins University Press, 1993.

Davis, B. G. *Tools for Teaching*. San Francisco: Jossey-Bass, 1993.

Jacobs, L. C., and Chase, C. I. *Developing and Using Tests Effectively: A Guide for Faculty*. San Francisco: Jossey-Bass, 1992.

Janzow. F., and Eison, J. "Grades: Their Influence on Students and Faculty." In M. D. Svinicki (ed.), *The Changing Face of College Teaching*. New Directions for Teaching and Learning, no. 42. San Francisco: Jossey-Bass, 1990.

Johnson, D. W., and Johnson, F. P. *Joining Together: Group Theory and Group Skills*. (4th ed.) Englewood Cliffs, N.J.: Prentice Hall, 1991.

McKeachie, W. J. *Teaching Tips: A Guidebook for the Beginning College Professor*. (8th ed.) Lexington, Mass.: D. C. Heath, 1986.

Marzano, R. and others. *Dimensions of Thinking: A Framework for Curriculum and Instruction*. Alexandria, Va.: Association for Supervision and Curriculum Development, 1988.

Meacham, J. "Discussions by E-mail: Experiences from a Large Class on Multiculturalism." *Liberal Education*, 1994, *80* (4), 36–39.

Sanders, N. M. *Classroom Questions: What Kinds?* New York: Harper & Row, 1966.

Stiggins, R. J., Rubel, E., and Quellmalz, E. *Measuring Thinking Skills in the Classroom*. Washington, D.C.: National Education Association, 1986.

Welty, W. M. "Discussion Method Teaching: How to Make it Work." *Change*, July/August 1989, *21*, 40–49.

White, E. M. *Teaching and Assessing Writing: Recent Advances in Understanding, Evaluating, and Improving Student Performance*. (2nd ed.) San Francisco: Jossey-Bass, 1994.

JOHN C. BEAN is a professor of English at Seattle University, where he directs the writing program.

DEAN PETERSON is assistant professor of economics in the Department of Economics and Finance at Seattle University's Albers School of Business and Economics.

Students need to develop oral presentation skills to function effectively in college and in the world of work. Professors can help students develop these skills by explaining how to design and assess presentations.

Designing and Grading Oral Communication Assignments

Brooke L. Quigley

Educators and employers are voicing a growing concern that college graduates do not possess the written and oral communication skills they need to be successful in today's workforce (Cronin and Glenn, 1991). According to recent surveys, employers report that an individual's ability to demonstrate effective communication in the workplace is the top skill or is among the top skills they seek in job candidates (Flaum, 1996). Practice in communicating an oral message is not only good preparation for employment, but also can be seen as fundamental to the educational experience (Modaff and Hopper, 1984; Steinfatt, 1986) and to preparation for civic responsibilities (Campbell, 1996). Clearly, the critical thinking skills required to create and convey an effective oral message are an important part of a college education. Yet many students have little, if any, structured practice or systematic assessment of their oral communication skills as part of their undergraduate programs.

Educators across disciplines can address their students' lack of these essential skills by including oral assignments as part of course requirements. Oral assignments can encourage an active, involved role in learning; enhance listening skills; promote articulation of ideas and opinions; provide opportunities to hear how others respond to one's thinking; and often provide practice in teamwork. Oral assignments also allow students to take greater responsibility for their own learning as well as learn significant course content from each other.

Educators in non–communication disciplines are obviously not expected to provide formal academic training in theories of communication or systematic teaching and assessment of oral skills. However, student skill development can still be addressed. In some universities, students receive practice in oral skills through communication-across-the-curriculum programs. In some programs, for example, communication faculty work closely with faculty in other disciplines, consulting in course development and design and assessment of oral assignments, teaching designated sections of non–communication courses, and/or providing individualized instruction through university-wide centers or laboratories (Cronin and Grice, 1993; Morreale, Shockley-Zalabak, and Whitney, 1993).

From a somewhat different perspective, this chapter provides guidelines for faculty on designing and assessing oral presentation assignments within their own courses. It offers suggestions for designing oral assignments, identifies general grading criteria that can be adapted for oral assignments, describes some ways to guide students in their preparation for speaking, and discusses some of the unique challenges that arise in the process of assigning and grading oral work.

Designing Oral Assignments

The type of oral assignment and the grading criteria depend, of course, on the academic discipline, the learning goals for the assignment, and the types of speaking expected of students who major in a professional area. Among the wide variety of skills that can be addressed through oral assignments are public speaking, fielding questions, giving feedback, interviewing, counseling, decision making, debating, negotiating, mediating, and resolving conflict.

Although there are various types of oral assignments, there are specific components that, in particular, speeches or presentations should address: purpose, audience, time, and questions. Instructors can design speaking assignments to bring out specified skills and may select from formats that simulate work, volunteer, or social tasks. The status report by a division head in a nonprofit organization, the proposal presented to prospective clients of a business organization, or the public speech or presentation assigned in introductory communication courses (Lucas, 1995; Nelson and Pearson, 1996; Osborn and Osborn, 1997) are examples of oral presentations that could serve as models for classroom assignments.

Several considerations concerning the design of oral assignments are identified in the following discussion.

Identify the Type and Purpose of Presentation.   Most student oral assignments are presentations that inform (share knowledge) or persuade (present a position for others to adopt). After determining the type of presentation, instructors need to encourage students to identify and state their own specific purpose within that framework. For example, a speaker may state, "My purpose today is to describe the rationale for the experiment, report the initial findings, and explain what needs to be done in the next phase. . . ." A clear statement of purpose guides the speaker, sets expectations for listeners, and identifies one criterion for assessment: Did the speaker achieve the purpose?

Identify the Audience for the Presentation.   During their careers, students will speak to numerous audiences, including coworkers, academic experts, and the general public. In each case, speakers must keep in mind their audience, and design their message for them. This is also true in the classroom. In most cases, it does not make sense to have a classroom assignment that is designed for an audience outside the classroom; the oral presentation should be designed for the classroom audience so that students get practice adapting to their listeners. The classroom audience will not only benefit from the information tailored to them but will also be able to provide feedback to the speaker about the effectiveness of the message.

Determine the Time Constraints.   Classroom oral presentations may range from a 3–5 minute short presentation to a 15 minute presentation. Typically an informative or persuasive speech is 6–8 minutes. Allowing another few minutes for the speaker to field questions adds up to about 12–15 minutes, a length of time that students are often given for presentations in other contexts. The time constraints for the assignment point to an additional grading criterion: Did the speaker create a message that fits appropriately within the time allowed?

Include Opportunities for Questions.   Students learn to "think on their feet" when assignments require them to answer questions following their presentation. Through this experience, students not only learn how clear or confusing they have been, but are often surprised to discover how capable they are at dealing with an unanticipated question. Fielding questions and comments is thus a useful requirement, typically expected in many business and professional contexts.

Explicating Grading Criteria

Communication instructors develop various sets of criteria for designing and grading their students' oral work. The general grading criteria are consistent with cultural expectations for public speaking: strength of the speaker's purpose and commitment, appropriateness of audience adaptation, effectiveness of reasoning, effectiveness of organization, and strength of extemporaneous delivery (Osborn and Osborn, 1997; Sprague and Stuart, 1996).

To assist students, instructors need to specify indicators for effective performance in these general areas. The assignment sheet presented in Exhibit 4.1 is an adaptation of several evaluation instruments that have demonstrated strong reliability and validity when used by multiple raters (Carlson and Smith-Howell, 1995). The form presented here is flexible because specific indicators can be modified depending on the assignment. The instructor can give a score and comments in each area, helping students to understand where, specifically, they are strongest in their speaking and where they need to improve. As students complete presentations and reflect on those assignments, they and the instructor may notice additional ways the assignment criteria could be modified or expanded, based on their own and their classmates' experience of speak-

Exhibit 4.1. Grading Criteria for an Informative Presentation

Name _____   Date _____

Topic _____   Grade _____

Introduction   (15 points)
The speaker gained audience's attention and interest.
The speaker stated the purpose and central idea of the speech.
The speaker gave a preview of the rest of the presentation.

Body   (40 points)
Audience adaptation:
The speaker tailored the message to audience interests.
The speaker used language and examples appropriate to audience.

Reasoning:
The main points were clearly and accurately presented.
The order of points was logical and easy to follow.
The main points were developed with appropriate detail and support.
The speaker used at least two outside research sources.

Organization:
The presentation had a clear introduction, body, and conclusion.
The use of transitions made the presentation easy to follow.
The speaker's written outline was correctly completed.

Conclusion   (15 points)
The speaker prepared listeners for the end of the presentation.
The ending summarized and pulled together the main points.
The ending reinforced the central idea of the presentation.

Delivery   (30 points)
The presentation was planned yet conversational in manner.
The speaker had frequent eye contact with listeners.
The use of notes was comfortable and unobtrusive.
The speech rate, clarity, and volume made the speech easy to understand.
The use of gestures reinforced the verbal message.
The speech was given in the time period specified (6–8 min.).
A visual aid, if needed, was used comfortably and effectively.

Additional Comments
Did the speaker achieve the stated purpose of the presentation?

ing. Through their peers' speaking, students see the grading criteria enacted; instructors can point to positive examples to reinforce grading criteria.

Guiding Students' Preparation

Instructors can clarify assignment expectations and guide student preparation in a number of ways, as discussed in the following.

Encourage Students' Curiosity.   The starting point for an oral presentation, as in a written assignment, is not necessarily library research but is the question or topic the speaker finds interesting. When students recognize that their own question is primary, they are less likely to become overwhelmed by the information they collect and are more likely to gain strength from their own sense of purpose. They are also more likely to be engaged and trust their own experience as one source of information relevant to their task (Campbell, 1996). For instance, a student interested in recycling needs to "discover" which aspect of the topic, perhaps a proposal of a campus recycling program, most interests her and may intrigue other students. Then the speaker can go to the library, the Internet, or to campus officials and begin researching the topic.

Promote Audience Adaptation.   As students prepare, they need not abandon their own interest, but they do need to tailor their interest and information to the audience, making the message interesting, relevant, and easy to follow. One way students can prepare is by having some class time to talk with other students about their topic. In a sense, speakers can "interview" other students or "try out" their ideas for making their topic interesting. Instructors can encourage their students to see preparation not as something done entirely alone or in secret, but as a process that includes getting feedback from actual audience members or others who are interested in the topic.

Assist in Organizing and Researching.   A defining characteristic of an oral presentation is that the audience usually has just one opportunity to understand the message; there are no instant replays. The message needs to be easy to follow, clear, understandable, and convincing the first time it is heard. Instructors can help students prepare carefully organized and reasoned messages by encouraging them to outline their presentations. At its most general level, a speech contains an introduction, a body with main points and elaboration or evidence related to each main point, and a conclusion. Those parts should be clear to the listener. Transitions, or "sign-post" phrases, such as "first," "second," and "finally," or "Now that we have looked at the cost of the program, let's examine some of the benefits, . . ." help the listener follow the logic of the message and understand it as a whole.

Students can select an organizational format that fits the topic. For example, a *sequential* design would be appropriate for a speech on photography that focuses on steps in the development process. On the other hand, a *causation* design would be better for explaining the causes that led up to a sudden decline in the stock market.

A strong organizational format also helps the speaker understand what kind of reasoning or support is needed to make the message convincing. Instructors can provide guidelines regarding the amount of research expected and the appropriate sources of information. Particularly in the case of persuasive messages concerning policy issues, such as a campus affirmative action policy, speakers need to critically evaluate their sources. Instructors can help students be more critical consumers of information by providing sets of questions students can ask themselves as they choose their sources of information.

Establish a Supportive Environment.   Instructors need to be aware that many students will be apprehensive about giving an oral presentation. An important way to address such concerns is to recognize that some anxiety is normal and to establish the class as a supportive learning environment. With leadership from instructors, students are very good at supporting each other by stressing the positive attributes of each others' work. It also helps for students to get to know each other in class and to practice together. If collegiality and peer practice are established early in the term, students have a better chance of managing the more challenging assignments and more pointed constructive criticism later. In addition, instructors can recommend a number of techniques ranging from systematic desensitization to positive visualization, to assist their students (Robinson II, 1997). Instructors can also provide special assistance to non-native speakers of English who are concerned about oral assignments (Quigley, Hendrix, and Freisem, 1998).

Offer Helpful Practice Strategies.   A number of strategies help students practice for oral presentations. First, students should be encouraged to practice orally, and to use the same notes during practice that they plan to use in class. This is not to say they should memorize or plan to read presentations. When students practice by memorizing whole speeches or by writing out their presentations, the results frequently sound like stilted speech or formal writing rather than natural, conversational speaking. While direct quotes or particular passages may be read, the bulk of the speech should be extemporaneous (planned yet conversational). In addition, speakers simply cannot judge how long a presentation will take unless they actually "talk it." Students who don't practice out loud are often the same students who think they don't have enough material to speak for five minutes and end up going over their allotted time.

Another strategy that helps students is to provide class time for them to practice giving the speech to a partner (Murphy, 1993). Students stand with their partners, all practicing at the same time in different parts of the classroom. While one student speaks, the other listens and is prepared to give feedback. With many students practicing at once, no particular student feels on display. The practice gives students a real opportunity to make themselves clear and get feedback about their speaking.

Finally, students can benefit by viewing examples of past students' speaking on videotape. Each term, instructors can ask students who gave exemplary presentations to agree to be videotaped for the benefit of future students (or to share their videotape if they are routinely recorded as part of their assignment). As examples are collected, instructors can create a library that is helpful to individual students and the class as a whole. After students view examples in class, it is important to discuss ways they saw the speaker meet the requirements of the assignment. If technology is available, all students can benefit from video-recording their speeches and reviewing them after class. Using video, students benefit by being in the role of a listener during their own speaking; they can then see how important it is for speaking to be adapted to the needs of listeners (Quigley and Nyquist, 1992). Viewing their own videos also encourages students to determine which elements of their speaking they want to improve.

Some instructors have students review their videos and write a short assessment of their specific strengths and areas for change.

Meeting the Challenges of Oral Assignments

Oral assignments create unique and important opportunities for students, but also create unique challenges for instructors when they grade the oral work. Among the challenges are hearing a presentation and grading at the same time, offering feedback that is constructive, and encouraging students to argue for their convictions. Several ways of meeting these challenges are discussed in this section.

Review the Presentation.   One challenge for instructors is the difficulty of paying attention to the presentation in class and simultaneously taking notes regarding the grade. Many instructors address this challenge by assigning grades in a two-step process. The first step is for the instructor to make initial comments on the assignment sheet during the presentation in class. To free themselves from the need to watch the clock, instructors can ask a student to use an unobtrusive stopwatch, accurately recording the length of the speech and effectively signaling the student at key intervals, such as holding up a flash card with the number "5" to indicate one minute remaining in a 6-minute presentation.

While instructors do the best they can to listen to the speech carefully in class, it is easy to miss key elements and is thereby advisable to listen to the speech again. Thus, the second step in assigning grades is to routinely video-record or audio-record the presentation in class, obviously with the students' knowledge. Instructors can then listen to the presentation again before assigning the final grade. Hearing the speech a second time, instructors can listen carefully for elements of the speech structure, the presence of transitions, details of information, and the logic or argument. Having the speech on audiotape or videotape also makes it possible for students to listen to the speech again with the instructor, if they have questions about their grade.

Give Constructive Feedback.   Some comments about the speech, offered by other students and the instructor, should occur right after the question period following the presentation. Such feedback is usefully framed in the language of what "worked" or "didn't work." For instance, a student might respond: "For me as a listener it really worked well when you compared the different designs of bridges in several well-known cities." It is essential to begin with the positive comments. Students hear that they have strengths in their oral communication and can build on those strengths. Comments concerning what "didn't work" or needs improvement are most useful when cast as constructive criticism of a specific element of the presentation. For example, a student might suggest: "It didn't work for me when you turned away from us for long periods when working with your flow chart—can you refer to the chart and still maintain frequent eye contact with the audience?"

Encourage Students to "Argue."   Finally, an additional challenge for instructors of classes where students give persuasive presentations is that students often are reluctant to give a presentation formed as an argument. That is, they are reluctant about or perhaps inexperienced at stating a position on a controversial issue and providing reasons and evidence that support their position. Students sometimes see this as coercion or "forcing" their views on others. The reality is quite the opposite. If students have done their audience analysis well, they know what type of argument or rationale would be most persuasive to their peers. Far from forcing their ideas on others, they are attempting to determine how to appeal to others. Students need to understand that their assignment reflects what is expected for any public speaker. Whether it's a presentation in engineering, a report in biology, or a speech in political science, the challenge is to address one's peers as effectively and persuasively as possible.

Conclusion

By assigning oral work, instructors can provide students with an opportunity to learn course content actively and to practice their presentation skills. The general guidelines discussed in this chapter are designed to help instructors in the planning, design, and assessment of oral assignments. When given oral assignments, students benefit from clear grading criteria, structured practice, and specific feedback. Students also benefit when instructors are prepared to overcome the typical challenges that accompany oral assignments. When instructors offer oral assignments with clear guidance and established grading criteria, students can become better prepared for the many tasks they will face in the workplace and in their communities.

References

Campbell, J. A. "Oratory, Democracy, and the Classroom." In R. Soder (ed.), *Democracy, Education, and the Schools*. San Francisco: Jossey-Bass, 1996.

Carlson, R. E., and Smith-Howell, D. "Classroom Public Speaking Assessment: Reliability and Validity of Selected Evaluation Instruments." *Communication Education*, 1995, 44, 87–97.

Cronin, M., and Glenn, P. "Oral Communication Across the Curriculum in Higher Education: The State of the Art." *Communication Education*, 1991, 40, 356–367.

Cronin, M. W., and Grice, G. L. "A Comparative Analysis of Training Models versus Consulting/Training Models for Implementing Oral Communication Across the Curriculum." *Communication Education*, 1993, 42, 1–9.

Flaum, D. "Internships, Right Major Help Grads in Job Hunt." *The Commercial Appeal*, May 12, 1996, p. C3.

Lucas, S. E. *The Art of Public Speaking*. (5th ed.) New York: McGraw-Hill, 1995.

Modaff, J., and Hopper, R. "Why Speech is 'Basic.'" *Communication Education*, 1984, 33, 37–42.

Morreale, S., Shockley-Zalabak, P., and Whitney, P. "The Center for Excellence in Oral Communication: Integrating Communication Across the Curriculum." *Communication Education*, 1993, 42, 10–21.

Murphy, J. M. "An ESL Oral Communication Lesson: One Teacher's Techniques and Principles." *Basic Communication Course Annual*, 1993, 5, 157–181.

Nelson, P. E., and Pearson, J. C. *Confidence in Public Speaking*. (6th ed.) Dubuque, Iowa: W.

C. Brown, 1996.

Osborn, M., and Osborn, S. *Public Speaking.* (4th ed.) Boston: Houghton-Mifflin, 1997.

Quigley, B. L., Hendrix, K. G., and Freisem, K. "Graduate Teaching Assistant Training: Preparing Instructors to Assist ESL Students in the Introductory Public Speaking Course." *Basic Communication Course Annual,* 1998, *10,* 58–89.

Quigley, B. L., and Nyquist, J. D. "Using Video Technology to Provide Feedback to Students in Performance Courses." *Communication Education,* 1992, *41,* 324–334.

Robinson II, T. E. "Communication Apprehension and the Basic Public Speaking Course: A National Survey of In-Class Treatment Techniques." *Communication Education,* 1997, *46,* 188–197.

Sprague, J., and Stuart, D. *The Speaker's Handbook.* (4th ed.) San Diego: Harcourt Brace, 1996.

Steinfatt, T. "Communication Across the Curriculum." *Communication Quarterly,* 1986, *34,* 460–470.

BROOKE L. QUIGLEY is assistant professor in the Department of Communication and instructional specialist for the Center for Academic Excellence at the University of Memphis.

Students' writing improves when instructors are clear and when students are included in the assessment process.

Designing and Grading Written Assignments

Eric H. Hobson

Informal and formal writing assignments have places in every course because writing provides students a unique learning process (Emig, 1977) and encourages active learning—a highly desired educational outcome (Bonwell and Eison, 1991; Hobson, 1996a). Additionally, writing helps establish and maintain disciplinary and professional communities (Russell, 1991); disciplines have much to gain and preserve by supervising students' introduction to the written discourse conventions that define professional communities.

Most commonly, disciplinary courses use writing for testing purposes, focusing on students' content knowledge, not their ability to communicate that knowledge. A disparity exists between the means and the ends for student communicative facility. Students are usually provided one "writing" course that purports both overtly and implicitly to certify students' writing competence. These courses are usually housed in English departments and, more often than not, provide structured writing instruction using the forms valued in that discipline—the literary essay, for example. English departments have abrogated responsibility for writing instruction elsewhere, and other departments ironically note students' inability to write in other valued genres: memoranda, legal briefs, lab reports, patient consult notes, and so on. When asked to address this imbalance by making writing part of *their* discipline's courses, however, faculty often respond, "My classes are too large," "I do not have time to read X number of papers," "Grading essays is too subjective," or "I'm not qualified" (Hobson and Schafermeyer, 1994, p. 423). While each of these statements holds some truth, the writing-across-the-curriculum literature attests to writing's role regardless of discipline, class size, class topic, or professors' feelings of insecurity as writers and writing coaches (Hobson, 1996b).

Evaluating writing is one of the biggest problems for professors of any discipline (White, 1994). To some extent, evaluating writing is subjective because, working independently or with common criteria, everyone grades uniquely: professors interpret grading systems to meet their intimate understanding of class context and goals, and such interpretations are condoned by institutions and disciplines. Comments about grading's "subjectivity" (usually meaning obfuscation) have merit, however, when considered from students' perspectives. Lackluster assignment construction contributes greatly to students' difficulties in completing assignments to their own satisfaction and that of their professors. Assignment construction also affects grading ease and reliability (White, 1994).

This chapter presents one of many assessment strategies pharmacy faculty use to grade student writing. The assignment and assessment process comes from a large (usually over eighty students) course, primarily lecture based, and taught by faculty with little or no experience in grading student writing.

Designing Writing Assignments

Students face many challenges in completing assignments:

- They must figure out the assignment's requirements (stated and unstated).
- They must identify an effective strategy or process to complete the activity.
- They must ascertain, as best they can, how the assignment will be evaluated.

Instructions about written assignments often are cryptic, such as, "Write an essay about X." Students are not told explicitly what document to create and rarely are specific guidelines provided that describe the expectations about citation formats, page formats, amount and type of research, and reporting structures. Instead, students are expected to be clairvoyant, to read professors' minds about how to best approach and complete assignments. Finally, they must parse out assessment practices: professors may well know their own expectations about end products at the start of an assignment, but they rarely share that information with students.

Many faculty shy away from requiring and assessing written documents as complete, multidimensional, rhetorical texts designed to persuade or inform an intended audience, choosing instead to evaluate one, limited textual domain—accuracy of information, or, more generically, "content." Although this choice is pragmatic, it is shortsighted. Evaluating written texts as one-dimensional entities does students a disservice by suggesting that their disciplinary community neither demands, values, nor rewards facility in writing. To suggest ways that faculty across the curriculum can grade student writing efficiently while also acknowledging the texts' complexities, I share the three steps pharmacy faculty used to recast an existing consumer's report writing assignment to achieve the following assignment characteristics:

- The assignment is carefully constructed and articulated.
- The assignment can be assessed quickly and consistently by multiple assessors (self, peer, and expert).

- The assignment instructions and assessment tools provide a model for other writing assignments.

Step 1: Revising the Assignment.   Faculty first discussed the assignment's existing, and fairly typical, instructions: "Write a 4–5 page review of a frequently used over-the-counter (OTC) or health-care product. You will be graded on accuracy of information and adherence to proper spelling and grammar usage." These instructions illustrate the hurdles that brief and cryptic instructions create for students. Because these were the only directions—except for due date—that students received, the students were left to ascertain the following critical issues—a risky proposition for novices: intended or appropriate audience for the report, appropriate format(s), evaluation areas to be emphasized, expected use of outside sources, and efficient process for completing the project.

Exhibit 5.1 contains the revised assignment with the assignment's purpose stated more clearly and the expectations for format, research process, and audience apparent from the start. The faculty's consensus at this point in the process was that the revised assignment would likely produce better final papers and reduce their evaluation time and anxiety.

Exhibit 5.1. Consumer's Report Instructions

Writing Assignment: OTC/Health Care Product Review
(Due: day, month, year)
Task and Purpose: Create a product review of a frequently used OTC or health-care product.
Audience: Specifically define the group of readers, determined by the author (for example, caregiver with feverish infant; adolescent male acne patient; geriatric female arthritis patient).
Format: Use the same format as an OTC patient education pamphlet or a magazine article such as those found in *Consumer's Reports* (see samples on reserve in library). Use graphics as needed to support the document's purpose.
Length: 1,000 word minimum

Overview
In this assignment, identify a product (preferably an OTC or health-care related product) that you use or will use in the near future, but that you should know more about in order to be an informed consumer. This assignment's aim is to allow you the time and guidance to thoroughly research your target product, to collate and synthesize the information you gather, and to create a consumer's report on this product.

A consumer's report is a product review intended to educate a particular group of consumers. It collects, reports, and synthesizes data relevant to the target audience's concerns and makes specific recommendations about if and how its audience should use a specific product. Effective reviews are thoroughly researched, usually using a mix of secondary and tertiary sources, and they are documented so that readers know where the information was collected and that it is reliable.

No product is designed and marketed for a general audience (even toilet paper companies design and market different products for specific groups of users). As someone providing a review and assessment of a product, you too must decide what particular group of users you are researching this product for so that you ask questions to gather the information your readers want. For instance, if you review orthopedic shoes, you would look at vastly different issues depending on whether you are presenting your information to 13-year-old boys or to their mothers. Although both groups would want to know the clinical viability of the shoes available, the boys would be concerned about whether they are available with a pump in a high-top model (that they could wear unlaced), whereas their mothers would want to know about their cost and durability.

Although these instructions are thorough, how the resulting paper is graded remained unclear. In the original and revised instructions, students were not briefed about how their texts would be graded; they submitted the report to have it returned with a grade noted on page one. Written comments noted grammatical, mechanical, or spelling mistakes, or highlighted errors of fact. It is understandable that students imagined themselves in a no-win situation and thus reconciled their grades by claiming, "I just didn't know what the professor wanted." In revising the assignment, faculty agreed that they should create common evaluation criteria for this and similar assignments, and that students need the criteria before they write. These conclusions echo assessment specialist Ed White's (1989) advice to make grading criteria explicit and public from the start.

Step 2: Creating Assessment Tools.   Faculty met several times to create assessment tools for the revised assignment. They reconciled their often divergent stances about what they valued in previous student responses and agreed on two points: they could create a set of assessment criteria they could all live with and use consistently, and students could benefit from formulating assessment criteria as a means to practice collaborating with peers and to understand and internalize the assignment's parameters and expectations. White argues that including students in the assessment process encourages them to "see the quality standards as partly of their own devising," and "since the standards for performance are clear and public . . . students are more ready to seek help in meeting them" (White 1989, p. 107).

Student-Based Assessment Activities

In light of this agreement, faculty created the following grading criteria task in which students (individually or in teams) analyze the assignment and past student performances, and articulate specific features that demarcate levels of success (see Exhibit 5.2).

Using student-generated criteria—whole or in part—requires professors to concede that students can articulate what distinguishes strong performances. The faculty team created a basic project peer-assessment tool (see Exhibit 5.3)

Exhibit 5.2. Criteria Development Activity

Project Evaluation Criteria Development

In the library's reserve section are four final projects. Review these reports and rank them in order of overall quality—decide which is best, next best, and so on.

For each report, identify specific characteristics that influence your ranking and explain in detail—refer to specific places in the report—why these characteristics establish the document's effectiveness.

Bring your rankings and explanations to class on [date]. We will use this information to establish specific guidelines and criteria for the final document. We will also describe what characteristics will define the levels of success the final projects may achieve.

You may want to meet with a Writing Center consultant who can be a sounding board for your ideas.

and encouraged individual faculty to incorporate student-generated criteria into the final rubric used to grade the projects.

Step 3: Using the Criteria to Grade Projects.   Originally the peer assessment form, with slight modification, was to serve as the project grading rubric. However, levels of comfort using the assessment criteria presented in Figure 5.3 varied, and many faculty wanted a more holistic rubric. To meet this need, faculty created a basic scoring rubric by which to adjudicate projects at each available grade option. Several found their students capable and willing to help modify and tailor the rubric and, in turn, students used this rubric, as well as the peer assessment form, to self-assess and revise project drafts (see Exhibit 5.4).

Faculty reported that revising the consumer's report assignment and developing the assessment rubric and related activities created a better-designed and more consistently evaluated project. They also commented that talking openly with colleagues about writing within their discipline and its evaluation reduced their anxiety about grading. Likewise, they believed that, given carefully crafted and explicit instructions, paired with access to evalua-

Exhibit 5.3. Project Peer Assessment Tool

Peer/Self Assessment Form

Task: Read your classmate's draft and apply the following criteria. In the blank before each statement, insert the score that you believe best reflects the draft's current state of development (Scores: +=Strong; O=Neutral; –=Needs work). On the back of this form, provide specific/detailed suggestions for revising the document to meet or exceed these criteria.

FOCUS
___ The report reviews a single, specific OTC or health-care product.
___ Thesis is clear and appropriately supported.
___ Author provides appropriate levels of basic and overview information
        (product history, uses, mechanics, costs availability, and so on).
___ Author provides detailed, documented information about benefits and detriments
        associated with product.
___ Distinguishes between objective and subjective data.
___ Uses objective and subjective data appropriately.
___ Compares similar products.
___ Review is well-developed: valid evidence and logical explanations support specific
        claims.

AUDIENCE
___ Author identifies and explains questions of central concernto the target audience.
___ Report meets a specific audience's information needs.
___ Author presents target audience therapeutically valid andspecific recommendations
        about product use.
___ Author is knowledgeable and objective about product.
___ Author clearly identifies and explains issues of concern fortarget audience.

PROFESSIONAL EXPECTATIONS
___ Documentation of information sources is accurate and thorough.
___ Grammatical, mechanical, typographic errors are rare.
___ Report fulfills all assignment requirements. .

Exhibit 5.4. Grading Rubric

Consumer's Report Grading Criteria

(A) Excellent

An excellent project presents a cogently planned, thoroughly researched, and clearly presented consumer's report. It anticipates and accommodates a specific audience's needs for various types of relevant and detailed information and raises no doubts in readers about the accuracy of its product assessment. The document contains no noticeable errors of fact or unbalanced treatment of source materials. It demonstrates mastery of the elements of effective writing.

(B) Strong

A strong project presents a well-developed review of a specific product, focusing on important features of the product and its use, discussing them in a generally thoughtful way. Its intended readers have little reason to doubt the accuracy of the information presented or the assessments made, although they may desire more detailed information and more thorough analysis. The document demonstrates good control of the elements of effective writing.

(C) Adequate

An adequate project presents a competent, albeit generic, product review. Information and analysis may be too general to meet the needs of a specific audience and/or the audience may be defined too generally to allow for specific product assessment and recommendations, leading the reader to desire more information to corroborate the document's assessment. The document demonstrates adequate control of the elements of effective writing.

(D) Limited

A limited project demonstrates some competence in creating a consumer's report; however, it may not identify or explain many of the following: intended audience, product use, analysis and recommendations made, sources used. Readers openly question the accuracy and reliability of information presented and the author's professional competence. The document is plainly flawed in its control of the elements of effective writing.

(F) Seriously Flawed

A seriously flawed project demonstrates serious weakness in creating a consumer's report; specifically, it fails to identify and explain one or more of the following: intended audience, product use, analysis and recommendations made, sources used. Because it is generally disorganized, underdeveloped, and subjective, the report provides little, if any, relevant or supported product information. Readers do not acknowledge the accuracy and reliability of information presented or the author's professional competence. The document demonstrates unacceptable control of the elements of effective writing.

tion criteria from the project's onset, students produced stronger reports than previously—a result that, by itself, made grading easier.

Parting Advice

Reformulating writing assignments as described here, although neither easy nor fast, is valuable. Consider the following advice about grading writing using assessment tools such as those outlined in this chapter.

It Takes Time and Energy.   Working solo or with colleagues to articulate assumptions about grading student writing and to formulate grading criteria can be difficult, time-consuming, and highly charged. Yet the investment pays dividends; as faculty settle into the routine of constructing and evaluating written assignments, they develop basic templates that apply to many activities and progressively reduce preparation time.

It Is Never Finished. Unlike test banks containing hundreds of multiple choice questions that can be shuffled, printed, and computer-scored, crafting strong writing assignments is a recursive process. Assignments are tweaked to reflect previous student responses, to acknowledge changes in a discipline's knowledge base, and to keep the assignments fresh and relevant. Assignments and assessment criteria may even need complete overhauls.

It Changes the Look of the Class Session. Incorporating explicit grading criteria, particularly criteria crafted in collaboration with students, requires devoting class time to discussing the activity itself and convincing students that they do play a role in assessment. Professors, however, rarely offer this role to students. This time must be made available if we think students deserve explicit instructions for written projects, multiple opportunities to ask questions about the project, as well as to receive formative feedback from several sources concerning students' attempts to complete the tasks.

It Is Worth It. Generally, grading writing is not painless; however, it can be a process that our students and colleagues believe is accurate and educationally beneficial. Although the specter of late-night grading sessions still looms menacingly, grading student writing that results from thoughtfully constructed assignments and clearly articulated evaluation criteria can make the task less dreadful, cumbersome, and disconcerting. More important, assigning and grading writing this way presents novice members of our disciplinary communities more accurate pictures of the purposes and value of writing in their education and careers.

References

Bonwell, C. C., and Eison, J. A. *Active Learning: Creating Excitement in the Classroom.* ASHE-ERIC Higher Education Report No. 1. Washington, D.C.: George Washington University School of Education and Human Development, 1991.

Emig, J. "Writing as a Mode of Learning." *College Composition and Communication,* 1977, *28,* 122–128.

Hobson, E. H. "Encouraging Self-Assessment: Writing as Active Learning." In T. E. Sutherland and C.C. Bonwell (eds.), *Using Active Learning in College Classes: A Range of Options for Faculty.* New Directions for Teaching and Learning, no. 67. San Francisco: Jossey-Bass, 1996a.

Hobson, E. H. "Writing Across the Pharmacy Curriculum: An Annotated Bibliography." *Journal of Pharmacy Teaching,* 1996b, 5 (3), 37–54.

Hobson, E. H., and Schafermeyer, K. W. "Writing and Critical Thinking: Writing-to-Learn in Large Classes." *American Journal of Pharmaceutical Education,* 1994, *58,* 423–427.

Russell, D. R. *Writing in the Academic Disciplines, 1870–1990: A Curricular History.* Carbondale: Southern Illinois University Press, 1991.

White, E. M. *Developing Successful College Writing Programs.* San Francisco: Jossey-Bass, 1989.

White, E. M. *Teaching and Assessing Writing.* (2nd ed.) San Francisco: Jossey-Bass, 1994.

Eric H. Hobson is assistant professor of English at Eastern Illinois University.

Evaluating students' collaborative work requires a variety of diagnostic and formative assessments.

Grading Cooperative Projects

Karl A. Smith

Successful cooperative group projects require an environment in which the conditions for joint project work and the requirement of a single product are carefully integrated and are seen as fair (and we hope beneficial) by the students. Many students have had unpleasant experiences working on poorly structured group projects. A common problem is that the workload is very uneven, so some students do most of the work while others do very little. Another common tension in group project work is students' uncertainty about how good is "good enough," since views about quality typically vary widely. Many problems related to cooperative projects can be eliminated through carefully structured groups and diagnostic, formative, and summative assessment. In essence, we must build quality into the process before assigning and grading cooperative projects.

Keys to Success in Cooperative Group Projects

The key to success in using cooperative group projects is to prepare yourself and the groups. The most important thing faculty can do to minimize problems in grading cooperative projects is to carefully structure the five basic elements of formal cooperative learning groups—positive interdependence, individual and group accountability, face-to-face promotive interaction, teamwork skills, and group processing. The professor's role in this process is first and foremost to make sure that there are good reasons for using the cooperative group work (complex task, multiple perspectives, divisible responsibilities, and so on), that there is sufficient time to complete the task successfully, that students possess the necessary skills and experience for successful group work, and that the instructional goals specify that a cooperative group or groups are required. If several of these conditions are met, then there is probably sufficient reason to use a formal cooperative learning group.

New Directions for Teaching and Learning, no. 74, Summer 1998 © Jossey-Bass Publishers

The professor's role in using formal cooperative groups involves the following steps:

1. Specify the objectives for the lesson.
2. Make a number of instructional decisions.
3. Explain the task and the positive interdependence.
4. Monitor students' learning and intervene within the groups to provide task assistance or to increase students' teamwork skills.
5. Evaluate students' learning and help students process how well their group functioned.

The basic elements and professor's role are presented in much greater detail with numerous examples in Smith and Waller, 1997; Smith, 1996; and Johnson, Johnson, and Smith, 1991.

Criterion-Referenced Assessment of Cooperative Group Projects

An underlying foundational requirement for successful use of cooperative learning is criterion-referenced assessment. Assessment is often done using norm-referenced grading, or "grading on a curve," rather than criterion-referenced grading, or an "absolute grading scale." In a norm-referenced grading scheme, students are compared with one another, lined up and given grades A-F relative to one another. In this scheme, no matter how good or poorly the students do in an absolute sense, there are fixed percentages of each grade category (10 percent A's for example). In a criterion-referenced grading scheme, absolute criteria are set (90 percent for an A, for example) and anyone and everyone who meets or exceeds this criterion receives that grade. In this scheme it is possible for everyone (or no one) to get an A.

Norm-referenced grading is often assumed to be the "norm" in higher education, but a national survey conducted by Astin (1993) indicates only about 22 percent of all faculty grade "on the curve." He noted that engineering faculty have the highest percentage of use of this scheme (43 percent), but that it is not used by the majority of faculty.

One of my favorite comments by Milton, Pollio, and Eison (1986) on norm-referenced grading schemes is, "It is not a symbol of rigor to have grades fall into a 'normal' distribution; rather, it is a symbol of failure—failure to teach well, to test well, and to have any influence at all on the intellectual lives of students" (p. 225).

The use of criterion-referenced evaluation is absolutely essential in classes where a high level of student cooperation is structured (group projects, for example). There is nothing more destructive than asking students to work together on projects (and perhaps share a grade) and then pit them against one another by grading them on the curve at the end. One of the most common reasons that cooperative learning, or more broadly, group work, fails is that faculty put students in a fundamentally incompatible situation—working together cooperatively and being pitted against one another at grading time. Perhaps this high percentage of "grading on the curve" is why many faculty have difficulty using cooperative learning.

Using a Variety of Diagnostic and Formative Assessment Formats

Grading students' projects is a summative assessment process. Faculty can ease the pain associated with that process by building in diagnostic and formative assessment.

We can learn a lot about students when they enter a course by having them complete a student information form. In my courses, during the first week of class, students complete a "course information form" on the Internet that surveys their expectations and motivations for the course and checks on their background and preparation. The previous course work of a student enrolled in a freshman engineering course is shown in Table 6.1.

Similar results were collected for a computer course: see Table 6.2. Seven students were most familiar with Macintosh computers, and twenty-three students were most familiar with IBM-compatible computers. Three reported that this is the first time they used the Internet; thirteen said they had used it a few

Table 6.1. Freshman Engineering Course, Fall, 1996

Level*	Probability	Statistics	Linear Algebra	Calculus	Analysis	Modeling
1	14	21	10	3	17	28
2	8	3	0	2	1	0
3	4	4	3	5	8	2
4	6	2	4	13	4	0
5	1	0	13	7	0	0

Key: (1) I have never had a course in this area, (2) I had a course but don't remember much, (3) I had a course and remember some of it, (4) I had a course and remember most of it, (5) I had several courses and remember most of them.

Table 6.2. Computer Course, Fall, 1996

Level*	Graphing Calculator	Email	Spreadsheet	Word Processor	Statistical Package	Program Language	Computer Algebra
1	1	3	4	0	26	12	22
2	2	11	11	0	2	9	6
3	8	4	14	6	0	7	1
4	19	12	2	24	0	2	1

Key: (1) I never have used one, (2) I know a little about them, (3) I have used them some, (4) I am very comfortable using them.

times; twelve said they could find their way around fairly easily; and two said they had their own web page.

At the end of the course, each student completes a review form using the Internet. All aspects of the course are surveyed, and this information is considered in revising the course for subsequent offerings. We also, of course, administer a standard form for students to evaluate teaching.

Another level of diagnostic assessment is building quality into the class through the use of continuous improvement processes, such as a student management team. A student management team is used by many faculty to operationalize Total Quality Management (TQM) principles. The operation of these teams is based on shared responsibility: "Students, in conjunction with their instructor, are responsible for the success of any course. As student managers, your special responsibility is to monitor this course through your own experience, to receive comments from other students, to work as a team with your instructor on a regular basis, and to make recommendations to the instructor about how this course can be improved" (Nuhfer, 1995, p. 3).

Typical attributes of student management teams are as follows:

- Teams are composed of three to four students plus a professor (I have had teams of up to twelve members in classes of eighty).
- Students have a managerial role and assume responsibility for the success of the class.
- Students meet weekly; the professor attends every other week. Meetings generally last about one hour.
- Team meets away from classroom and professor's office.
- Students maintain log or journal of suggestions, actions, and progress.
- Team may focus on the professor or on course content.
- Team utilizes group dynamics approach of TQM.

The members of the student management team meet weekly and distribute the minutes of the meeting via email to the teaching team and, when appropriate, to the entire class. Members take turns facilitating the meeting and recording the minutes. A representative of the team reports to the class each week.

Many problems typically encountered by faculty using groups may be eliminated or lessened through careful structuring of the groups and the professor's expectations of the groups. Carefully designed assessment plans also lead to success.

Assessment of Cooperative Group Projects

There are three principal phases—before, during, and after the lesson—in the design of assessment plans for cooperative group projects. Before the lesson, evaluation criteria such as those listed in Exhibits 6.1 through 6.3 must be developed. Be sure to inform students of the criteria, preferably in the course syllabus. Plan how to collect information on students' progress. Define the

Exhibit 6.1. Group Project Report Evaluation Form

Category	Possible Points	Points Received	Comments
Executive summary	20		
Problem	10		
Method	10		
Results	20		
Discussion	20		
References and appendix	10		
Organization Cover page Table of contents	10		
Total	100		

Exhibit 6.2. Dichotomous Scale for Evaluating Writing

	Yes	No		
Substance	___	___	1.	Paper addresses the issue.
	___	___	2.	Paper has a focus, a central idea.
	___	___	3.	Paper develops major aspects of the central idea.
	___	___	4.	Paper shows awareness of importance of main ideas.
Organization	___	___	5.	Structure or pattern of the paper is clear.
	___	___	6.	Paper has an introduction, development, and conclusion.
	___	___	7.	Each paragraph is coherent.
	___	___	8.	Transitions from one idea to next are logical.
Mechanics	___	___	9.	Sentence structure is coherent.
	___	___	10.	Sentences are not awkward.
	___	___	11.	Sentences are varied.
	___	___	12.	Errors in use of verbs are few.
	___	___	13.	Errors in use of pronouns are few.
	___	___	14.	Errors in use of modifiers are few.
	___	___	15.	Errors in word usage are few.
	___	___	16.	Punctuation errors are few.
	___	___	17.	Spelling errors are few.
Evidence	___	___	18.	Statements are accurate.
	___	___	19.	Opinions are adequately supported.
	___	___	20.	Sources are identified and documented appropriately.
Mechanics (alternative)	___	___		Paper shows control of grammar.
	___	___		Paper shows control of syntax.
	___	___		Paper has few misspellings.

Exhibit 6.3. Persuasive Argument Composition Rubric

Name: _____ Date: _____

Title of Composition: _____

Scoring Scale: Low 1–2–3–4–5 High

Criteria	Score	Weight	Total
Organization: Thesis statement and introduction Rationale presented to support thesis Conclusion logically drawn from rationale Effective transitions		6	(30)
Content: Topic addressed Reasoning clear with valid logic Evidence presented to support key points Creativity evident		8	(40)
Usage: Topic sentence beginning every paragraph Correct subject-verb agreement Correct verb tense Complete sentences (no run-ons or fragments) Mix of simple and complex sentences		4	(20)
Mechanics: Correct use of punctuation Correct use of capitalization Few or no misspellings		2	(10)
Scale: 93–100 = A; 87–92 = B; 77–84 = C			(100)

process of learning, especially the number and type of iterations permitted on students' work.

During the lesson, observe and sample groups, or interview individual students. In addition, collect interim group products or informal products such as "minute" papers, a one-minute opportunity for students to write a response to a particular issue.

After the lesson, collect the group product and evaluate it using the format and rubrics outlined before the lesson began. A single product, such as a group report, is a common part of cooperative group work. The procedure I use for reviewing and grading cooperative group projects is a table such as the one reproduced in Exhibit 6.1. A copy of this form is included in the syllabus along with specific suggestions for items to include in each section.

In addition to using a clearly defined grading form such as the one in Exhibit 6.1, it is also important to provide rubrics indicating what you're looking for in each of the categories. This information is also included in the syllabus in my courses. A simple, dichotomous scale for evaluating writing from Moss and Holder (1998) is presented in Exhibit 6.2. A more complex rubric from Johnson and Johnson (1996) for grading a persuasive argument composition is presented in Exhibit 6.3.

Making Assessments Meaningful

According to Johnson and Johnson (1996) three components lead to meaningful assessment: (a) significant purpose, (b) student involvement, and (c) future learning.

To be Meaningful, Assessment Must Have a Purpose That Is Significant. For instance, assessment should give students and other stakeholders accurate and detailed feedback both on the process students are using to learn and the quality and quantity of their learning. Assessment should also improve learning and instruction.

Assessments Are Meaningful When Students Are Involved in Conducting the Assessment. In meaningful assessments students understand the assessment procedures, invest their own time and energy in making the assessment process work, take ownership of assessing the quality and quantity of their work, and want to share their work and talk about it with others.

Meaningful Assessments Provide a Direction and Road Map for Future Efforts to Learn. Meaning is created through involvement that leads to commitment and ownership. Professors must ensure students are involved in these five steps for making assessment meaningful:

1. Setting learning goals
2. Planning how to achieve their learning goals
3. Determining progress and success in achieving their goals

Assessment results help students

4. Take pride and satisfaction in their efforts to learn.
5. Set new learning goals and repeat the first four steps.

Assigning Students' Grades

Most faculty who make extensive use of cooperative learning use a combination of group and individual assessment. I have done show-of-hands surveys of hundreds of faculty during cooperative learning workshops that revealed that the percentage of individual students' grade based on the evaluation of group work typically ranges from 5 to 20 percent. Some faculty use higher percentages in project-based courses, such as senior design projects in engineering. For example, Exhibit 6.4 shows grade breakdown from a recent senior-level civil engineering class I taught.

Conclusions

Assessment, especially grading, is fraught with problems, and the grading of cooperative projects is no exception. Indeed, it adds more complexity. These

Exhibit 6.4. Grade Breakdown in Civil Engineering Course

Grades will be based on the following:

Group	Maximum
Group Projects (4 at 100 points each)	400 points
Final Examination	100 points

Individual	
Homework (10 points each)	50 points
Midquarter Examination 1	100 points
Midquarter Examination 2	100 points
Brief Reviews (2 at 25 points each)	50 points
Heuristics Project	75 points
Review or Application Project/Paper	125 points

Course Grades:

A 900 points and above
B Between 800 and 899 Points
C Between 700 and 799 Points

A grade of **D** or **F** is available upon request. Although students will be given grades of **I** if necessary, it is highly discouraged. Absolutely no incompletes will be given for uncompleted group work.

problems are not new, but have been debated throughout the history of education. The problems inherent in giving students grades have led some to study grading and marking (Becker, Geer, and Hughes, 1995), others to advocate abandoning grades (Sager, 1995), and has led many others to advocate focusing on learning and not on grading (Deutsch, 1985; Smith, 1986). Cooperative learning is an extraordinarily effective way to help students learn (Johnson, Johnson, and Smith, 1991) even in science, math, engineering, and technology (Springer, Stanne, and Donovan, 1997). Grading cooperative projects, although challenging and difficult, can, if done carefully, help students and faculty reap the benefits from and with one another through cooperative interaction.

References

Astin, A. W. "Engineering Outcomes." *ASEE PRISM,* 1993, *3* (1), 27–30.

Becker, H. S., Geer, B., and Hughes, E. C. *Making the Grade: The Academic Side of College Life.* New Brunswick, N.J.: Transaction Press, 1995.

Deutsch, M. *Distributive Justice.* New Haven, Conn.: Yale University Press, 1985.

Johnson, D. W., and Johnson, R. T. *Meaningful and Manageable Assessment Through Cooperative Learning.* Edina, Minn.: Interaction Book Company, 1996.

Johnson, D. W., Johnson, R. T., and Smith, K. A. *Active Learning: Cooperation in the College Classroom.* Edina, Minn.: Interaction Book Company, 1991.

Milton, O., Pollio, H. R., and Eison, J. A. *Making Sense of College Grades.* San Francisco: Jossey Bass, 1986.

Moss, A., and Holder, C. *Improving Student Writing: A Guidebook for Faculty in All Disciplines.* Dubuque, Iowa: Kendall/Hunt, 1988.

Nuhfer, E. B. *A Handbook for Student Management Teams.* Denver: Office of Teaching Effectiveness, University of Colorado at Denver, 1995.

Nuhfer, E. B. "Student Management Teams: The Heretic's Path to Teaching Success." In W. E. Campbell and K. A. Smith (eds.), *New Paradigms for College Teaching.* Edina, Minn.: Interaction, 1996.

Sager, C. *Eliminating Grades in Schools: An Allegory for Change.* Milwaukee, Wis.: ASQC Quality Press, 1995.

Smith, K. A. "Cooperative Learning: Making 'Groupwork' Work." In C. Bonwell and T. Sutherlund (eds.), *Active Learning: Lessons from Practice and Emerging Issues.* New Directions for Teaching and Learning no. 67. San Francisco: Jossey-Bass, 1996.

Smith, K. A. "Grading and Distributive Justice." In L. P. Grayson and J. M. Biedenbach (eds.), *Proceedings of Sixteenth Annual Frontiers in Education Conference,* IEEE/ASEE. Arlington, Tex., 1986.

Smith, K. A., and Waller, A. A. "Cooperative Learning for New College Teachers." In Campbell, W. E. and Smith, K. A. (eds.), *New Paradigms for College Teaching.* Edina, Minn.: Interaction, 1997.

Springer, L., Stanne, M. E., and Donovan, S. *Effects of Cooperative Learning on Undergraduates in Science, Mathematics, Engineering, and Technology: A Meta-Analysis.* Madison, Wis.: National Institute for Science Education, 1997.

KARL A. SMITH is associate professor of civil engineering at the University of Minnesota.

Special problems and opportunities related to assessment and technology are illustrated. Examples are given of assessing students' use of technology and assessing the products they create with technology.

Evaluating Technology-Based Processes and Products

Gary R. Morrison, Steven M. Ross

Educators have seen many new technologies during the past century, ranging from lantern slides to films with sound, teaching machines, television, and computers. Most recently, the Internet has both infiltrated and enhanced classroom instruction. College professors have often embraced these technologies in search of innovative means of teaching, and as these technologies filter into the classroom, their applications for instruction grow as faculty adopt them. Each technology presents new opportunities for learning, but also new challenges for evaluating its use.

The increasing influence of cognitive and constructivist theories of learning on instruction have significantly expanded the perspectives applied by educators in developing and evaluating uses of technology for instruction (Ross and Morrison, 1995). Today, the traditional testing focus on isolated knowledge and skills (see Grady, 1992) is expanding to include evaluation of meaningful performance in using technology as an applied tool. For example, current trends in education suggest the use of open-ended learning environments, such as problem-based learning, which produce a different type of learning experience and product than is produced in the traditional learning environment (Barrows, 1985; Land and Hannafin, 1997; Savery and Duffy, 1995). Open-ended learning environments as well as other constructivist approaches encourage the use of authentic tasks based on real-world problems that are often mediated by technology (Cognition Technology Group at Vanderbilt, 1992; Honebein, Duffy, and Fishman, 1993; Jonassen, 1991). The learning resulting from such an approach is not easily assessed with a traditional paper-and-pencil test but requires evaluation that is geared to the real world and grounded in performance standards. Using holistic scoring procedures or rubrics, for instance, potentially increases the reliability of assessing such complex performances and the richness of information provided to students regarding their level of achievement (Jonassen, 1991; Taylor, 1994).

This chapter focuses on assessing students' use of technology and the products they produce using technology. Although we involve students in many applications of technology, we have selected two examples, representing diverse subject matter and processes, to examine here. One deals with assessing student listserve responses in a technology seminar course. The other involves using technology to analyze and interpret data in a statistics course.

Technology-Based Products

To assess a technology-based product, we must first determine what we are assessing. Students can use technology as both a process (means) and a product (end). An example of using technology as a process or means is the use of a word processor to create a research paper. In most cases, we are interested in assessing the content of the paper and possibly the format of the paper, if students are required to follow a particular style guide. The assessment of the paper would not focus on students' use of the word processor, but on the final product. However, when technology is used as a product or end, our assessment focus is on the use of the technology as well as on the product. For example, a project in an instructional design class requiring the development of a computer-based instructional (CBI) unit or a web-based course would focus on both the use of the technology and the product produced by the technology. Thus, the evaluation would assess the use of the technology by considering the quality of animations (for example, speed and smoothness), sound quality, compressed video quality, answer input and judging methods, and quality of cross-platform delivery. Evaluation of the product would include the visual design, the content, and the instructional strategies employed. Similarly, an evaluation of class discussion conducted by listserve might include an evaluation of students' use of the technology (for example, appropriate email etiquette, timeliness of response, and correct use of the technology) while the product produced by the technology, (for example, listserve messages) might focus on the content of the messages and behaviors exhibited in the messages (such as supporting, disagreeing, or extending other posts to the listserve). Our focus in the remainder of this chapter is on both the process of using the technology and the product produced by the technology. We will examine assessment techniques for class participation on a listserve and in a computer-based data analysis project.

Assessing Listserve Discussions

As Internet access grows and connecting becomes easier, faculty are finding new ways to use Internet technology in the classroom. One strategy we have used was the implementation of a listserve in a graduate seminar. An eight-week summer course on theories influencing instructional design models posed many problems at an urban university, including conflicts with job travel, family obligations, and vacations. One viable solution was to conduct the class via a listserve. Thus, rather than meeting one evening a week for a discussion of a topic, the class discussion was conducted via a listserve. Each Monday, the two students responsible for leading the week's discussion posted initial ideas and questions. For the next six days (and 24 hours a day!) all the class members and the two professors discussed the topic by posting email messages to a listserve, resulting in asynchronous communication. One advantage for the students was the ability to attend a softball or soccer game scheduled during normal class times. A disadvantage was not reading email for a few hours on a given day; the thread of the discussion could change more than once while people were away from their computers. The grade for the course consisted of an assessment of each student's postings to the listserve, reaction papers, and a research paper. All papers were posted on the course web site, which required a password for admittance. The following discussion describes a rubric we developed to assess the student postings to the listserve.

Discussion on a Listserve.   Professors have routinely assigned points for participation in class discussions; however, these discussions are typically limited by a time block assigned to the class meeting. Traditional classroom discussions are easy to follow because students use a protocol and generally stay on one topic. The discussion ends with the end of the class meeting or when the instructor changes to a lecture or some other activity. A discussion on a listserve is quite different. For example, Bob might create a rather lengthy post that expresses his opinions on several topics (for example, a behavioral approach versus a cognitive approach and how to use each in an at-a-distance course). Karen might respond only to the behavioral approach in Bob's message. Lonny might disagree with Bob's interpretation of constructivism, and Dave might ask questions about the appropriateness of the techniques for pacing in a distance learning course. The discussion has now grown from one thread (behavioral versus a constructivist approach in distance learning) to three new threads. In a matter of hours or even minutes, the listserve discussion can grow into several simultaneous threads that tax anyone's ability to follow each. The complexity of these discussions and the lengthy time frame pose unique problems for the faculty member who needs to assess individual contributions to the discussion as part of the course grade.

Selection of Postings.   A problem with grading a listserve discussion is selecting which email messages or posts to evaluate. In a recent course, for example, the number of posts per student ranged from 3 to over 170, with most of the students posting approximately 35 messages (about 6 per week). The two students with the most posts (more than 150) were often commenting to one another, but made significant contributions to the discussions with their more serious replies. Rating six messages a week for six students is a manageable task. The problem was determining which messages from the two most vocal students to rate. An analysis of the postings showed a clear distinction between posts directed at the discussion and those that were more commentary or quips between the two students. One possibility, then, was only to assess the posts directed at the discussion and ignore the other comments. A second method was to take a random sampling of all posts by all students, especially if there are a large number of postings. If proper listserve and discussion etiquette are part of the course objectives, then the instructor may need to limit or control the off-task comments by deducting points or some other strategy (such as sending private email to the offender).

One approach to evaluating contributions is to use a rubric (see Exhibit 7.1) to assess either all or a sampling of the posts to the listserve. This rubric for assessing listserve discussions consists of four constructs that receive individual ratings.

The first construct focuses on mechanics—the grammar and composition of the post. Students are expected to use grammatically correct sentences that are free of spelling errors. The four levels of the rubric allow us to rate the posts according to organization, grammar, and spelling. We found a tendency for some students (and ourselves) to become lax about grammar and spelling. In addition, knowing that one's posts are rated on grammar and spelling might encourage a student to read the post to correct errors and refine the organization *before* sending the message.

The second construct is participation in the discussion. Students are expected to contribute at least five postings per week to the list and to discuss the topics with all the class members rather than one or two selected individuals.

The third construct is the content of the post. Each post should exhibit a high level of understanding of the discussion unless the post is asking for clarification. The rating that best describes the individual message for each construct is selected.

The last construct is a rating of the critical thinking evidenced by the posting. Students are expected to critically examine several topics during the course and to discuss both their views and those of others on the listserve. The rubric provides a means for rating the postings based on the depth of knowledge indicated by the post (for example, has the student read the required readings, or simply skimmed information from other posts?).

The selected postings to the listserve are rated on the four constructs and then summed for a total score. An instructor can also create two scores from the rubric. The sum of the mechanics and participation scores describes the students' use of the technology (in other words, the email, software, spell checker, and listserve access). The sum of the content and critical-thinking ratings provides a score based on the subject content. An instructor teaching a computer literacy course that focuses on the use of email and listserves might give more weight to the technology score whereas an instructor teaching an honors history course might give greater weight to the content of the discussion.

Assessing a Computer-Based Data Analysis

This section describes the assessment of a computer-based project in an introductory statistics course for graduate students in education. The course is

Exhibit 7.1. Rubric for Evaluating a Discussion Conducted via a Listserv

Mechanics of Posting   Rating _____

Points

4   Complete sentences, well organized, grammatically correct and free of spelling errors

3   Complete sentences, well organized, but some (2 or fewer) grammar and/or spelling errors per paragraph

2   Complete sentences, comprehensible, organization could be improved to present a more coherent argument or statement, has 3 or more grammar and/or spelling errors per para graph

1   Poor sentence structure, inadequate organization, several grammar and/or spelling errors per paragraph

Participation in Discussion   Rating _____

Points

4   Provides comments and new information regularly (for example, during each discussion day) and equitably; interacts with a variety of participants

3   Provides comments and some new information fairly regularly (for example, during three-fourths or more of the discussion days); interacts with a few selected participants

2   Sporadically (for example, responds during one half or less of the discussion) provides com ments and some new information; interacts with only one or two participants

1   Provides one or two responses during the discussion

Content of Posting   Rating _____

Points

4   Reveals a solid understanding of the germane topic as evidenced by thoughtful responses and questions

3   Reveals an adequate understanding of a germane topic as evidenced by posts indicating superficial knowledge

2   Reveals a restricted understanding of a germane topic limited to information that could be derived from prior posts

1   Message is unrelated to discussion

Critical Thinking Evidenced by Posting   Rating _____

Points

4   Offers a critical analysis of an existing idea (posted or published) or introduces a different interpretation to an existing idea

3   Agrees or disagrees with existing discussion and provides limited justification/explanation

2   Agrees or disagrees with existing discussion but provides no justification/explanation

1   Provides no evidence of agreement or disagreement with existing discussion

Total Points _____

required for all doctoral students and for some master's students pursuing a variety of majors in the college of education at a large urban university. The course is taught in the evening to a class of approximately thirty students, most of whom hold full-time jobs and have limited opportunity to use university resources (such as the library and computer laboratories) during regular business hours. Students' skills in and attitudes toward mathematics and statistics vary considerably.

Grading in the course is based on multiple assessments, including a midterm and final examination (each 100 points), a computer exercise (30 points), and a computer data analysis project (50 points). The latter activity, which is the focus of this section, is designed as a relatively authentic measure of students' abilities to subject realistic data to statistical analysis, interpret the output, and describe the results and conclusions in an 8–12 page research report. The data project is oriented toward a study involving a comparison of three treatment groups. The nature of the study and the preparation is fully described for students, as if they were data analysts who were being consulted after the study was performed. Students then receive a unique set of data and are trained to use a PC-based statistical application package. The complexity and open-endedness of the task create challenges for grading the projects in a meaningful and valid manner. Some of these challenges are as folllows:

- Students may run the data analysis program correctly, but use the wrong statistics.
- Students may run the correct statistics, but interpret them incorrectly.
- Students may run and interpret the statistics correctly, but not write the report clearly or in the appropriate style or depth.
- On any of these performance dimensions, students may do some parts of the project well and other parts below standards.

These considerations led to the development of the scoring rubric shown in Exhibit 7.2. The scoring rubric awards an overall grade (within a point range) based on a holistic evaluation of the product relative to described performance expectations (for example, accurate analyses and interpretations). Within each category, additional points can be earned (designated by a '+') for higher-level performance in report writing. The rubric is shown to students and discussed at the time the project is formally assigned.

An essential part of the evaluation procedure is providing two types of written comments on students' report. *General* comments are used to highlight the overall impression of the project and justify the grade awarded (for example, "Well-written report and very clear interpretations of the analyses you used"). *Specific* comments that refer to particular content of the report (for example, "You should have used a chi-square test here; correlation implies an interval or ordinal variable," or "Your reporting of the analysis of variance results was very thorough and understandable"). An important component of this grading procedure is the provision of feedback in addition to the infor-

Exhibit 7.2. Rubric for Computer-Based Data Analysis in Graduate Statistics Course

Category	Description
(5+)	(Same as 5, but report is well-written with highly in-depth interpretations.)
5	All correct analyses; interpretations exceed standards in depth, with no errors on report. Overall quality of the report is good, but not exceptional (writing, presentation, and so on).
(4+)	(Same as 4, but report is well-written with in-depth interpretations.)
4	All correct analyses; interpretations are nearly all correct, but include some errors. Report is adequate, but not superior in content or writing quality.
(3+)	(Same as 3, but report is well-written with in-depth interpretations.)
3	Mostly correct analyses; some errors or limited interpretations on report. Report is adequate, but not superior in content or writing quality.
(2+)	(Same as 2, but report is well-written with an attempt at in-depth interpretations.)
2	Mostly correct analyses, but mostly incorrect or limited interpretations. Report is adequate but not superior in content or writing quality.
1+	(Same as 1, but report is well-written with an attempt at in-depth interpretations.)
1	Mostly incorrect analyses; mostly incorrect or limited interpretations. Report is adequate or minimal.

Point Conversion Scale

Rating	Points*
5	45–50
4	40–44
3	35–39
2	30–34
1	0–29

*Within a category, a "+" raises the score from the minimum level of the interval (for example, 30, 35, 40, 45) by a variable amount not to exceed the maximum score level.

mation in the rubric. The combination of written comments with the rubric provides a more complete assessment and direction for the student.

Advantages and Disadvantages of Rubrics

The rubrics and evaluation system used in our classes for technology-based processes and products seem effective thus far. One indication of their success is that no student has yet complained about his or her grade. All students seem to like knowing exactly how their project or postings will be evaluated before they start their work. When they receive their grades, in the form of a category rating (1–5+) and points (0–5), they seem to better understand and accept how the grades were derived than did students in previous classes. As students better understand the use and importance of rubrics, they may use rubrics to prepare their products either through self- or peer evaluation. For example, a student might use the criteria from the rubric to identify essential parts of a paper (for example, problem statement, hypotheses, and so on). Similarly, a student might use a rubric to determine whether a project includes all the elements identified by the rubric and to make necessary changes before submitting the paper or project. Another advantage is a perceived increase in the validity of grading. The "scores" derived seem less subjective and are linked much more directly to clear criteria than are grades assigned holistically and not associated with defined performance levels. Thus, we plan to continue to use and modify the evaluation system in similar assignments in other courses.

We have experienced few disadvantages. One, perhaps, is the time involved in devising the rubric, but the dividends, as just described, seem much greater than this cost. Another is that not all performances clearly seem to fit in only one level of the rubric. Here, as in conventional grading (but to a lesser degree), a subjective decision should be made about the best fit. We have also found instances where a student completed a project with a high rating on the rubric, but the project was very mechanical (by the book) in nature. Although we hesitate to add a category titled "creativity," we are trying to develop an assessment category to distinguish between projects that simply follow the rules versus projects that exhibit creativity and unique approaches.

The major implications of the uses of rubrics are increased appreciation by us, our students, and more gradually, other faculty about the advantages of alternative grading strategies. Many of our colleagues, for example, assign project grades by subjectively deciding what level (A, B, C, and so on) is most appropriate given the overall "feel" or "impression" of the work. These individuals will probably find, as we have, that students exposed to rubrics are less accepting of traditional evaluations because they want to know clearly the qualities of their products and how a performance level, or grade, was assigned, given those qualities. A second important implication is exposing our students—future professors, instructional designers, evaluators, and educational researchers—to effective use of rubrics and alternative assessments. Experiencing the use of rubrics as a student can help these students develop an understanding of rubrics' applications and provide a foundation for students' using rubrics in their work environments.

Conclusion

The assessment of technology-based products requires the instructor to determine whether the assessment will consider (a) only the use of the technology, (b) only the product produced by the technology, or (c) a combination of the technology use and the product. This question is best answered by considering the objectives for the course or project. For example, an introductory research course might allow partial credit for generating a computer-based statistical analysis even though there were errors in the commands for the analysis. An advanced research course, though, might require a correct statistical analysis and award credit only if the analysis is correct. Partial credit, however, would be offered for an accurate but incomplete interpretation of the data. Thus, each instructor must determine the focus of the assessment and the emphasis that the technology and product are given.

References

Barrows, H. S. "A Taxonomy of Problem-Based Learning Methods." *Medical Education*, 1985, *20*, 481–486.

Cognition and Technology Group at Vanderbilt. "The Jasper Series as an Example of Anchored Instruction: Theory Program Description, and Assessment Data." *Educational Psychologist*, 1992, *27*, 291–315.

Grady, E. *The Portfolio Approach to Assessment*. Bloomington, Ind.: Phi Delta Kappa Educational Foundations, 1992.

Honebein, P., Duffy, T. M., and Fishman, B. "Constructivism and the Design of Learning Environments: Context and Authentic Activities for Learning." In T. M. Duffy, J. Lowyck, and D. H. Jonassen (eds.), *Designing Environments for Constructivist Learning*. Berlin: Springer-Verlag, 1993.

Jonassen, D. J. "Evaluating Constructivist Learning Environments." *Educational Technology*, 1991, *31*, 28–33.

Land, S. M., and Hannafin, M. J. "Patterns of Understanding with Open-Ended Learning Environments: A Qualitative Study." *Educational Technology Research & Development*, 1997, *45*, 47–73.

Ross, S., and Morrison, G. R. "Evaluation as a Tool for Research and Development: Issues and Trends in Its Application to Instructional Technology." In R. D. Tennyson and A. E. Barron (eds.), *Automating Instructional Design: Computer-Based Development and Delivery Tools*. New York: Springer-Verlag, 1995.

Savery, J. R., and Duffy, T. M. "Problem-Based Learning: An Instructional Model and Its Constructivist Framework." *Educational Technology*, 1995, *45*, 31–38.

Taylor, C. T. "Assessment for the Measurement of Standards: The Peril and Promise of Large-Scale Assessment Reform." *American Educational Research Journal*, 1994, *31*, 231–262.

GARY R. MORRISON is professor at Wayne State University, where he teaches courses in instructional design.

STEVEN M. ROSS is professor in Educational Psychology and Research at the University of Memphis and editor of the research section of Educational Technology Research and Development.

Portfolios provide an opportunity for students to participate actively in their learning by selecting materials for their portfolios and engaging in self-assessment.

Portfolios: Purposeful Collections of Student Work

Joan A. Mullin

Portfolios can be defined simply as a collection of students' work over a particular period of time. This may include drafts, previously graded assignments, in-class tasks, as well as formal texts or projects. However, as portfolio use has developed, the emphasis has shifted from just collecting various projects for assessment according to an instructor's criteria, to what Paulson, Paulson, and Meyer (1991) have called "a purposeful collection of student work that exhibits the student's efforts, progress and achievements in one or more areas . . . [which] provides a complex and comprehensive view of student performance in context. It is a portfolio when the student is a participant in, rather than the object of, assessment" (pp. 60–63).

Student participation within the assessment process proves to be the most significant factor in the increased use of portfolios. This chapter addresses the benefits of portfolios for students, the portfolio assessment process, the advantages and challenges of using portfolios, and the future of portfolio assessment.

The Benefits of Portfolios for Students

Much of the literature on portfolios addresses their use in writing classrooms (for example, see Bell, 1992; Lamme and Hysmith, 1991; Metzger and Bryant, 1993; Murphy, 1994; Valeri-Gold, Olson, and Deming, 1991/1992). However, portfolios have become a means of evaluation in a variety of disciplines, including mathematics, social sciences, and education (Frazier, Palmer, Duchein, and Armato, 1993; Gay, 1991; Larson, 1991; Wolf, 1989).

Faculty from a variety of disciplines have identified benefits of using portfolios. For instance, they agree that portfolios

- Demonstrate both the process of learning over time as well as the products of learning (Ballard, 1992; Cooper and Brown, 1992; Wolf, 1989)
- Encourage students to reflect on their own progress as learners and participate in the evaluation process (Ford, 1993; Stahle and Mitchell, 1993; Valeri-Gold, Olson, and Deming, 1991/1992)
- Develop collaborative capabilities among students (Cooper and Brown, 1992; Wiggins, 1989)
- Emphasize the development of student self-esteem and problem-solving (Cooper and Brown, 1992; Metzger and Bryant, 1993)

Another benefit, according to Wiggins (1989), is that portfolios respond to the call for "authentic" assessment. He explains that authentic assessment provides evaluations that "replicate the challenges and standards of performance that typically face writers, business people, scientists, community leaders, designers, or historians." Wiggins further asserts, "[L]egitimate assessments are responsive to individual students and to school contexts," noting that a legitimate assessment "is most accurate when it entails human judgment and dialogue" (pp. 703–704).

An additional benefit of using portfolios is that they provide a means for addressing problems of fairness in grading and provide insight into students' performance. For instance, portfolios can indicate (1) the amount of work students have been willing to engage in, (2) the thinking processes they used to transform information over time, (3) their ability to revise their work based on peer and instructor corrections and suggestions, and (4) their development in a discipline. Mostly, portfolios can unmask for students and faculty the processes of learning that are well hidden in traditional assessment methods. In particular, portfolios encourage student participation, foster collaboration, and enhance student self-esteem.

Student Participation.   With traditional assessment practices, students depend on teacher evaluations of their capabilities and seldom are given opportunities to critically self-assess. What self-assessments they do engage in are largely derived from an instructor-provided rubric. Their own critical self-assessment skills are not actually employed except inasmuch as they fit into another's set of criteria and values. Portfolio assessment, however, can provide opportunities for students to use self-assessment to determine how well they have succeeded at meeting not only their instructor's criteria, but also goals they have set for themselves.

Studies agree that student involvement in the creation of criteria by which they will be evaluated promotes effective learning because "[f]or them, evaluation is no longer a mysterious process conducted by some external agent; it is something they can do for themselves. They are internalizing standards and judging for themselves the quality of their work" (Brown, 1989, p. 32). For example, students display in their end-of-the-term reflections a critical ability that runs deeper than the abilities they usually have a chance to display. On one such reflection, a student wrote, "I didn't like the paper on which I received an A. It was easy for me to write. I really liked the B paper because it was a subject I was interested in, but it was difficult to write. . . . That paper made me really think hard and write in a way I had never written before: objectively, but about myself. I guess I was still in the thinking stages when I had to hand it in, but I like it the most, and in many ways, I think it was my best paper" (composition portfolio assessment, 1991, University of Toledo).

In addition, when students use their own rubric to reflect on their portfolios, they report seeing for the first time how much work they did. A student realizes, "I really learned a whole lot more that I thought!" In fact, students report that the challenge of sorting through their collected material is an invaluable one when portfolios are used either for capstone experiences or individual classes. For example, Frank Spicuzza (1996) examined the benefits of portfolio assessment for senior social work students and found that students were "reviewing assignments in the introductory social work courses and comparing them to the more advanced work completed in their upper division classes. The process enabled the seniors to reflect on their strengths and weaknesses as entry-level social workers, their changing interest in and perceptions of social work practice, and their need for continual development" (p. 5).

Portfolios encourage students to participate in the evaluation process, and thus, students have a greater stake in their own learning and assume more responsibility for it.

Collaboration.   Another benefit of the use of portfolios is that students and the instructor work collaboratively throughout the semester. Examples of this collaboration might include determining what type of portfolios will be required, the format for the portfolio, what documents contribute to the portfolio, and how the portfolio will be graded. One way to include students in the evaluation process is to have them participate in creating rubrics, so that students learn to collaborate with each other and professors. The cooperative class effort sets the stage for students to

- Translate together the instructor's goals, objectives, and standards into meaningful language for themselves
- Begin planning as a group how the goals, objectives, and standards will determine how the class will approach the task of assessment
- Reveal to others their own assumptions, expectations, and goals about the course

Perhaps the most valuable reason for creating criteria collaboratively is that questions about procedures and concepts emerge prior to the task itself. In the case of portfolio assessment, students can (1) seek clarification of class material or objectives, (2) determine together the value placed on surface features, such as grammar, sentence structure, and the visual impact of a text, as compared to the value placed on content, (3) question whether surface features and content should be separated, and (4) learn to use various formats by writing reflective responses in the form of a letter, an essay, or a checklist. When students create rubrics, they reach consensus about what is valued in the class, and they are held accountable to the group's decision.

Self-Esteem.   Another benefit of students' involvement in collaborative self-assessment is that it increases not only their motivation to learn, but also promotes their "intellectual autonomy and self-respect" (Adams and Hamm, 1992, p. 104). Leslie Ballard (1992) witnessed this when her students struggled over two days to assess their portfolios. She noted that they approached this task with more intellectual autonomy and self-respect than she'd seen before: "I had seldom seen students write with such intensity. Students who always complained about trying to come up with five-hundred words were suddenly writing four to seven pages when no length requirement was imposed. Others whose writing had been plagued throughout the semester with mechanical errors handed in papers with few if any such problems" (p. 48). This points to the relationship between students' participation in their own assessment and their enhanced self-esteem.

In general, when students understand the goals and purposes of a task, and participate in establishing and using criteria to assess their work, they are motivated to excel. Self-assessment also enables students to develop "basic competencies for professional practice and additional confidence for future professional development" (Spicuzza, 1996, p. 5). Such self-assessment, Spicuzza continues, enhances students' "self-esteem and their appreciation of the breadth and depth of their educational experience."

Portfolio Assessment Process

To motivate students, the instructor can employ various assessment strategies that enable students to participate actively in the portfolio evaluation process. Even though portfolios can be assessed in various ways, any assessment should take into account these five guiding questions, according to Valeri-Gold, Olson, and Deming (1992, pp. 299–300):

> What kind of structure will the portfolio have?
> What evidence will it contain?
> When will the instructor/students assess the work?
> How will the instructor/students assess the work?
> What will happen to the portfolio at the end of the term?

Structure of Portfolios.   The following example illustrates a highly structured portfolio. The instructor makes essentially all the decisions about the portfolio except the criteria and the kind of evidence students will include in the portfolio.

The instructor begins by outlining several specific objectives and the means by which proficiency will be determined. For example, suppose an English instructor wants each student to be able to recognize and analyze particular genres, demonstrate an ability to create a thesis that produces a critical analysis of various works, and cogently support the thesis in various kinds of written forms. To achieve the objective, she might set up portfolio guidelines asking students to (1) give examples of writing in three different genres, (2) include all the draft stages of at least one paper, and (3) include eight journal entries about their readings to demonstrate their analytical abilities. She also might ask the students what kinds of evidence they would want to include in the portfolio to represent ways in which they have learned course materials and demonstrated proficiency.

Portfolios also can be less structured. For instance, in each of my classes, some team-taught, the goal of the course is compacted into one central question that students' portfolios must address for the course:

Art/English. Can you visually and textually explain "visual literacy"?

Art History. As a member of the medieval team assigned the responsibility to design the [sculpture program, windows, or blueprint, for example] how did your process lead to both difficulties and successes?

Sociology. If you were to start a grassroots organization, how would you ensure your success?

Readings in Biology. Explain how the readings in the area we studied differ from other readings you encounter. What does that tell you about the profession?

Geography. What is the relationship between population and geography? Should we spend time determining this, or are our resources better spent elsewhere?

Writing. What is "advanced writing"? From what point do you advance and where do you end up?

Portfolio Evidence.   When I use less structured portfolios, I give students the "operative question" at the beginning of the semester. Throughout the course we discuss the evidence they might collect and how it will be assessed. Students' three-ringed binders might contain assigned papers, drafts of their writing, journal entries, in-class response papers, examples of writing from popular or professional media, and samples of their own writing from other classes or from other periods of their lives. Toward the end of the term, we devote a day to work on the portfolio. Students arrange their materials so that they can answer the operative question. In addition, they must write an introduction, explaining to me how I should interpret the evidence. Their reflection statements also include a self-assigned grade based on how well they have answered the operative question through their work in the class.

Development of Criteria.   During the first part of the semester, lively class discussions enable students to begin identifying assessment criteria. This process proves instructional for both students and the instructor. For example, students might ask, How am I already measuring up to my obligations in this class? I might ask, What assumptions are students operating under? How can I better instruct or guide students in their learning?

At various times throughout the semester, students are given in-class time to discuss criteria in groups. Each group reviews how well the criteria are working and presents its reasoning to the class. I write the groups' ideas on a master sheet, and we use this sheet to construct the final assessment rubric. Because students have been creating grading criteria for their other assignments and because we have discussed their portfolios, I seldom need to add my own criteria to their list; students are able to target the important goals in the class. Although this takes class time, it is instructional in that the operational question (the goal of the course) is continually being discussed.

Self-Grading.   The process of self-grading a portfolio encourages students to look at all the work they've done for the semester, organize it into evidence for an argument (that is, what their grade should be in relation to the class question), and use their own evidence to construct an analysis that will argue for their position. Their honesty is telling: "I didn't like this course so I didn't put much work into my papers, and it shows. But you can see that I enjoyed writing the paper on futurists. I think it shows that I can write a persuasive paper if I put my mind to it—I just didn't have the time or energy for this class. However, I did try near the end and you can see a noticeable improvement from the Rifkin paper on: I'm more organized, I took care with the spelling and grammar, and I was able to give better examples to support my arguments. While I'm sure I didn't produce the best papers in the class, I think I should get a C for improving as I did" (University of Toledo student portfolio, 1990).

By the time students arrive at this stage, having assessed their portfolios at mid-term also, they know the value of the work they have produced. They are able to assess the amount of work they put into the course as well as the amount of worth they got out of the course.

Other Assessment Strategies.   Faculty may wish to draw on other portfolio assessment strategies. For example, Ballard's English students assessed their portfolios according to the following guidelines (1992, p. 46):

1. The students rank their papers in order of most to least effective, with a brief rationale for what they think are the good and bad points and what they have learned though the assignment.
2. They discuss what they have learned about writing as a result of the course and the way they write.
3. They describe how they feel about writing at this point and compare their current view of writing to their view before they took the course.

A different assessment strategy is used by Knight in a mathematics class. Knight (1992) has students choose five examples from all their work that "represented their math knowledge and effort" (p. 71). No matter how students' responses are structured, though, the central purpose is to have students review their materials and present a self-evaluation that indicates their learning during the term.

Advantages and Challenges of Using Portfolios

As noted throughout this chapter, there are numerous advantages to using portfolios. Primarily, portfolios

- Emphasize "[p]roduction rather than recognition. . . . Students must demonstrate competence rather that selecting (or memorizing and repeating) an answer" (Calfee and Perfumo, 1993, p. 532).
- Urge students to assume responsibility for their own work and to critically and collaboratively assess themselves. "As students learn to work cooperatively they expand their knowledge, horizons, and possibilities and build their knowledge of themselves and the world" (Adams and Hamm, 1992, p. 105).
- Provide data for short- and long-term studies at the student, classroom, and curricular levels (for example, see Stahle and Mitchell, 1993).

The portfolio process actually gives students opportunities to demonstrate both that they have learned and that they are capable of learning. Portfolios provide professors a window on instruction that is not offered by other assessment methods. For instance, did most students find a particular concept difficult? Was there one paper at which everyone succeeded or failed? Why? What made that task accessible or inaccessible for most students? Was the task too easy or too difficult? Was your preparation as an instructor adequate? How close did most of the class come to meeting your objectives? Should you stretch course goals or otherwise revise them? Do you agree with the students' self-assessments? Did you reach your own goal of sharpening their critical skills?

Portfolio collections and their assessment emphasize students' performance and application, rather than knowledge. Portfolios can assist professors in diagnosing and understanding student learning difficulties, including problems with growth in ability, attitudes, skill development, expression, and the ability to collaborate with others. Because they assess student progress over time, portfolios can help students improve their learning and help professors improve their teaching (Adams and Hamm, 1992, p. 103).

However, problems and challenges also are associated with portfolios. For instance, managing the collection of materials can be a headache. Asking students to bring their portfolio materials to each class can be burdensome. They may also resent it if they bring their materials to class but are not given class time to work on them.

Another challenge associated with portfolios is related to power and control. Sometimes professors find it difficult to suspend their expectations and share class control with the students. Conversely, students initially may not believe they can assume responsibility for their own assessment because they are not used to such accountability.

Another problem is time. Professors have to be willing to take time in class to answer questions about portfolios and give students time to work on them.

Likewise, the amount of time spent on actually reading the portfolio can be mitigated by reading primarily the students' own assessments, but evaluation may well take much longer than a Scantron machine takes to read an answer sheet for a final exam. Professors seek time-efficient assessment because of real pressures in their lives, but as Black, Helton, and Sommers (1994) point out, tests and other quick assessments with their easy, simple results work against students assuming more responsibility for their assessment.

The Future of Portfolios

Professors are already developing cyber portfolios of student work and web pages that serve as links to students' research and thought processes. For many professors across the university, portfolios are flexible enough to serve their purposes and those of the curriculum, and portfolios meet the current call for authentic assessment of students' skills and performance. Portfolios also hold the potential for being adapted to future institutional and community assessment needs.

References

Adams, D. M., and Hamm, M. E. "Portfolio Assessment and Language Studies: Collecting, Selecting, and Reflecting on What Is Significant." *Social Education*, 1992, *56* (2), 103–105.

Ballard, L. "Portfolios and Self-Assessment." *English Journal*, 1992, *81*, 46–48.

Bell, S. "Portfolios and Paulo Freire's *Pedagogy of the Oppressed*: A Descriptive Analysis." *Teaching English in a Two-Year College*, 1992, *19*, 95–96.

Black, L., Helton, E., and Sommers, J. "Connecting Current Research on Authentic and Performance Assessment Through Portfolios." *Assessing Writing*, 1994, *1* (2), 247–267.

Brown, R. "Testing and Thoughtfulness." *Educational Leadership*, 1989, *46*, 31–33.

Calfee, R. C., and Perfumo, P. "Student Portfolios: Opportunities for a Revolution in Assessment." *Journal of Reading*, 1993, *36* (7), 532–538.

Cooper, W., and Brown, B. J. "Using Portfolios to Empower Student Writers." *English Journal*, 1992, *81*, 40–45.

Dodd, A. W. "Issues to Consider When Scoring Student Portfolios." In S. Tchudi (ed.), *Alternatives to Grading Student Papers*. Urbana, Ill.: NCTE, 1997.

Ford, M. "The Process and Promise of Portfolio Assessment in Teacher Education Programs: Impact on Students' Knowledge, Beliefs and Practices." In T. Rasinski and Padak (eds.), *Inquiries in Literacy Learning and Instruction*. Kent, Ohio: College Reading Association, 1993.

Frazier, D., Palmer, P., Duchein, M., and Armato, C. "Preservice Elementary Professors' Evolving Perceptions of Portfolio Assessment." In D. Leu and C. Kinzer (eds.), *Examining Central Issues in Literacy Research, Theory and Practice*. Chicago: National Reading Conference, 1993.

Gay, P. "A Portfolio Approach to Teaching a Biology-Linked Basic Writing Course." In P. Belanoff and M. Dickson (eds.), *Portfolios: Process and Product*. Portmouth, N.H.: Boynton/Cook, 1991.

Knight, Pam. "How I Use Portfolios in Mathematics." *Educational Leadership*, 1992, *49* (8), 71–72.

Lamme, L. L., and Hysmith, C. "One School's Adventure into Portfolio Assessment." *Language Arts*, 1991, *68*(8), 629–640.

Larson, R. "Using Portfolios in the Assessment of Writing in the Academic Disciplines." In P. Belanoff and M. Dickson (eds.). *Portfolios: Process and Product.* Portsmouth, N.H.: Boynton/Cook, 1991.

Metzger, E., and Bryant, L. "Pedagogy, Power and the Student." *Teaching English in a Two-Year College,* 1993, *20,* 279–288.

Murphy, S. "Portfolios and Curriculum Reform: Patterns in Practice." *Assessing Writing,* 1994, *1* (2), 175–207.

Paulson, F. L., Paulson, P., and Meyer, C. "What Makes a Portfolio?" *Educational Leadership,* 1991, *48,* 60–63.

Spicuzza, F. "An Evaluation of Portfolio Assessment: A Student Perspective." *Assessment Update,* 1996, *8,* 4–6.

Stahle, D., and Mitchell, J. "Portfolio Assessment in College Methods Courses: Practicing What We Preach." *Journal of Reading,* 1993, *36,* 538–548.

Valeri-Gold, M., Olson, J., and Deming, M. P. "Portfolios: Collaborative Authentic Assessment Opportunities for College Developmental Learners." *Journal of Reading,* 1991/1992, *35,* 298–304.

Wiggins, G. "A True Test: Toward More Authentic and Equitable Assessment." *Phi Delta Kappan,* 1989, *70,* 703–713.

Wolf, D. "Portfolio Assessment: Sampling Student Work." *Educational Leadership,* 1989, *46,* 35–39.

JOAN A. MULLIN is director of the Writing Across the Curriculum Program and the Writing Center at the University of Toledo and is coeditor of The Writing Center Journal.

Inquiry projects have not been easy to evaluate within the parameters of academic grading systems. Rubric-guided assessment of inquiry projects is discussed in this chapter along with the advantages and problems associated with this approach.

Grading Inquiry Projects

Beverly Busching

Academic disciplines are defined not only by bodies of knowledge but also by ways of knowing—by interpretive frameworks and methods of investigation. Merely mastering a knowledge base does not mean one is educated in that field; education in a discipline involves engaging in investigations to create knowledge in ways particular to that discipline. Intellectual communities can be viewed, in fact, as networks of individuals who engage with others in the field in "a common search for meaning" in their work or academic lives (Westerhoff, 1987).

In this chapter I focus on student assignments that consist of this search for meaning. I use the term *inquiry project* to refer to these assignments, although they take many different forms—some formal in nature, others more casual. The common elements are that students formulate and pursue questions of personal interest using multiple sources of information and, usually, multiple investigative methods. Concepts from the particular discipline (or course) provide a framework for the methodology and findings.

Involving students in inquiry projects has come to be viewed as a critical component of learning in many fields of higher education (Mishler, 1990; Smagorinsky, 1996). These investigations make visible the methodology, values, and intellectual stance of the discipline. They reveal to students their own knowledge in ways that only the *use* of knowledge in real settings can offer, and they demonstrate in powerful ways how knowledge is used in a field (Schon, 1987). Additionally, the integration of personal purposes with academic learning is critical in assisting career decisions and creating early initiation into professional roles and commitments.

Inquiry projects, so desirable from the standpoint of student commitment and learning, have not been easy to evaluate within the parameters of academic grading systems. As an example of one solution to this problem, I describe an approach to grading used for an inquiry project that I have assigned over the past four years in several classes. Exhibit 9.1 shows the handout that describes this project.

New Directions for Teaching and Learning, no. 74, Summer 1998 © Jossey-Bass Publishers

Exhibit 9.1. Guidelines for Inquiry Project: Pursuing Questions in a Self-Selected Area of Literacy Teaching

This is your opportunity to learn more about an area of English or language arts that interests you. Perhaps this is an area of instruction that you feel passionate about or an approach that uses your special talents. Perhaps it is an area of uncertainty for you. Possible topics include the following: listening to and writing poetry, emergent literacy, storytelling, teaching and learning grammar, author studies, literature study groups, writing in science or math, the authoring cycle, service learning, non-standard English.

Inquiry Stance: Letting First Questions Lead to Others

Begin with what you wonder about. This might be called the "messing around" stage. Read a little bit or talk to someone who has experience with this subject. Then formulate some questions to guide your search and write them in a notebook where you will collect your information as you go. As you learn more, modify and add to your questions, and write them down.

Sources

In your search, use at least three difference sources:

1. People who know about this topic
2. On-line sources
3. Professional journals. For example, journals such as *Reading Teacher, Language Arts, Primary Voices, Voices from the Middle*

Another good source of information is primary data, gathered by observing, interviewing, or involving yourself in an experience.

Products (Turn in with Your Self-Assessment)

1. Write a revised and edited paper 4–7 pages in length that communicates in a compelling manner your search and the most important information that you found. Have a conference with another student before your final draft. See handout on I-Search papers for a suggested organizational format and samples.
2. Create a set of 3–4 lesson plans or other instructional products that fits your I-search topic.
3. Write a bibliography with sources in APA format as provided in class materials or another format that you prefer. Interviews are listed in a section called Notes. On-line sources are listed in a section with that title.

Reference: Macrorie, K. The I-Search Paper: Revised Edition of Searching Writing. Portsmouth, N.H.: Boynton/Cook Heinemann, 1988.

Do a search—not research—in which the job is to search again what someone has already searched. But do an original search to fulfill a need, not that the teacher has imagined for you, but one that is important to you.

Rubric-Guided Assessment of Inquiry Projects

A rubric is a guide for qualitative judgments about student work that provides both criteria and standards of attainment for those criteria. Using a rubric to guide grading tells an instructor what to look for and what kind of work represents various levels of attainment, thus increasing consistency of judgment and explicitness of standards. In the project described here, I wrote only the criteria areas on the scoring guide; standards of attainment were developed in discussions with the class.

The rubric I am using as an example (Exhibit 9.2) is based on my study of the nature of inquiry in the learning of professional practitioners in my field, through library research (for example, Cochran-Smith, and Lytle, 1993; Macrorie, 1988; Daiker and Morenberg, 1990), and by analyzing my early experiences with student inquiry projects.

When I first began assigning inquiry projects, I gave continual feedback and direction as students progressed from decision to decision, but I did not communicate a preset rubric in advance. The better students were comfortable with this loose guidance, but it was an uncomfortable process for me and for the less confident students. I view this period of discomfort as an inevitable accompaniment of change. I had to become more proficient in my under-

Exhibit 9.2: Rubric for Inquiry Project Assessment

Processes of the Inquiry

10   Pursuit of questions is evident and shows commitment to topic.

20   Sources are sufficient, valid, and diverse.

10   Draft of paper shared with a response partner.

Name _____

Written/Created Products

20   Content is substantive and shows inquiry processes and your most significant findings in a conceptual framework.

10   Formats selected to communicate your learning are appropriate.

10   Written work is edited for clarity and standard written English.

10   Bibliography in appropriate form is included.

Overall Assessment

10   Principles of learning from Masters of Education classes are evident.

____   Possible extra points: Other characteristics, such as creative product, unusual sources, or innovative format, are present.

standing of a very complex process of learning before I could judge student products with preset criteria.

The rubric shown in Exhibit 9.2 was created to give weight to the critical processes of investigation while preventing the uncontrolled factors of working in a real-world environment from counting against the student. Interviews, observations, and other sources of information that depend on other people in businesses, schools, or homes are not always predictable.

The major characteristics of the rubric are as follows:

Both performances and products are assessed. The processes most critical to inquiry are emphasized in the grading criteria: personal investment in topic; appropriate, sequential, and multiple investigation strategies; valid and multiple sources; multiple drafts of final paper with a revision conference; and self-analysis of inquiry strategies. The products are judged based on substantive content with clear guiding concepts, professionally appropriate materials, clear writing, careful editing, and appropriate bibliography. Another item applies to all aspects of the project: evidence of application of learning from the course.

Criteria categories are weighted in a point system to give more weight to the most critical criteria.

No levels of attainment or definitions of categories are given because, having class twice a week during the project, I involve the students in discussions to define criteria and standards based on sample projects and material from class.

The rubric defines the major aspects of inquiry and is closely tied in language and sequence to descriptive handouts for the project.

Both student self-assessment and professor assessment are included. Because of the idiosyncratic nature of these projects, leeway is given for additional qualities of students' work that may not be included in the generic rubric.

Practical considerations include leaving space for students' and my comments under each criterion and including no more items than will fit on one page.

Rationale for Rubric-Guided Assessment

At every level of education, assessment has evolved toward more valid ways to evaluate students' thinking and their use of knowledge in authentic applications (Andrew and others, 1996; Davies, Cameron, Politano, and Gregory, 1992; Stiggins, 1997; Wilkinson and Silliman, 1997). The use of rubrics has emerged as a critical component of this movement (Carroll, Potthoff, and Huber, 1996; Stiggins, 1997).

Rubrics accompanied by demonstration products assist in communicating clearly to students the basis for judgments that lead to a grade on performances and products (Charney and Carlson, 1995). Research in college classes shows that the basis for grading is often not clear to students, and faculties lack a firm theoretical, discipline-wide basis for adjudicating between different interpretations of student texts (Elbow and Belanoff, 1991; Newkirk, 1984). With a rubric and sample papers that explicitly define the criteria on which evaluation is based, professors can reach reasonable levels of consistency (for example, Hughes and Keeling, 1984). Experience itself, even without systematic training, leads to greater reliability (Sweedler-Brown, 1985).

Lack of explicitness has particularly profound consequences for marginal students, contributing to their continuing failure (Rose, 1989). Inquiry projects themselves can be a powerful force to integrate the personal aims of students from nonacademic backgrounds into academic pursuits (Herrington and Curtin, 1990).

Once students feel they understand the rubric (see next section), the extent to which students feel that evaluation is an outside force imposed on them is greatly reduced, although inexperienced student inquirers will inevitably be uncertain about how the process will unfold. Students can take over the assessment process, monitoring what and how they are doing as they work. The confidence to decide for oneself what to value in an ambiguous situation fuels assertive learning. Confident that they know my expectations, students are free to make their own judgments and to do what inquiry does best—broaden perspectives and generate new questions and problems (Dysthe, 1996; Short and Burke, 1991).

Using the Rubric to Teach and Assess

The rubric is given to students in advance, along with a narrative description of purposes and criteria (see Figures 9.1 and 9.2).

I teach students the form of the paper, using high-quality journal articles based on similar kinds of inquiry and also student papers from former years. We read through these articles together, speculating about the research processes that created them, and noting the decisions the author appeared to make in selecting content to be included and in organizing that content. If more assistance in writing is needed, I hold individual conferences and loan students books on writing such as Zinsser's *Writing to Learn* (1988) and *On Writing Well* (1990) and Macrorie's *The I-Search Paper* (1988).

I teach students to revise and to hold peer conferences that assist revision. Donald Murray's (1978) article on revision is invaluable for students who avoid review because they believe that only poor writers have to revise. Murray presents a compelling case for revision describing it as what good writers do to their best thoughts to make them even better.

Students are taught to give each other conferences that focus on clarifying and expanding the content. First, the respondent tells the writer what is strongest about the content so the writer can build on strengths. Then the respondent asks questions to clarify information and main points, and, using the rubric, to identify missing requirements. These conferences are positive in tone and very helpful in directing the writer's revisions. The process of peer assessment makes the criteria more salient and helps students gain insight into project requirements.

Brief, small-group sessions to share project plans and to tentatively apply one or two dimensions of the rubric are also part of the process of teaching the criteria. Students share ideas about the performances that would or would not satisfy criteria, and I respond to their ideas. Finally, students hand in their own final assessment of their project with the final paper.

Advantages and Problems of This Rubric

The weighted rubric grading approach corresponds to the complexities and uncertainties of the inquiry process, and it permits students to engage in the critical decisions of inquiry without penalty for pursuing some unproductive trails. It is an assessment approach that supports the best efforts of students and at the same time helps me teach. It provides me with a clear rationale for my grading and reduces my unintended bias in qualitative judgments. Students rarely question a qualitative grade backed up with a rubric they understand. Even more, the rubric assists me in being an ally and a coach who helps students meet criteria. The rubric, though time-consuming to construct, enables me to grade long papers more quickly.

Modifications and Extensions

I am continually working to improve my processes of creating shared understanding of the rubric with the class. I have made a video of a student from last year describing her project, and I hope that this will encourage neophyte inquirers to envision what the project entails.

I could perhaps create descriptions of levels of performance, although the great variations inherent in inquiry make this difficult. I have been looking at other rubrics of performances and complex products (see Claggett, 1996, for example) and may find something that I can adapt to my needs. A scoring guide for inquiry projects is appropriate for every discipline, but must be adapted to the nature of investigation in each discipline (Jolliffe, 1985; Mathison, 1996).

The clear specification of criteria in rubrics can provide the basis for conversations about grading among professors. At my university, "teaching breakfasts" have been instituted to create this kind of dialogue across colleges. At Syracuse University, the faculty in the writing program are working toward shared practice through such exchanges among a mixed group of full-time research faculty, part-time professional writing professors, and graduate teaching assistants. They hope to reduce great inconsistencies in grading practice in the program. Bishop (1991) suggests that the use of grading rubrics can also be used to train new professors.

Conclusion

I am committed to engaging students in decisions and judgments that expand their interpretive framework and their commitment to their profession. Very simply, they learn so much more if they work in ways that mirror how one learns in the field. As one student reported in her course evaluation, "I feel I now have a cohesive grasp of [this subject]. I really liked the flexibility to do what I wanted. At first I thought this was just another assignment to do, but once I got going, I really enjoyed thinking more about [it]. . . . It made me consider things I wouldn't have known were an issue."

I have found rubric-based assessment to be a tool that allows me to integrate inquiry projects into my courses.

References

Andrew, M., and others. "Predicting Performance in a Teaching Internship." *Journal of Personnel Evaluation in Education,* 1996, *10,* 271–278.

Bishop, W. "Going Up the Creek Without a Canoe: Using Portfolios to Train New Teachers of College Writing." In P. Belanoff and M. Dickson (eds.), *Portfolios: Process and Product.* Portsmouth, N.H.: Boynton/Cook, 1991.

Carroll, J. A., Potthoff, D., and Huber, T. "Learnings from Three Years of Portfolio Use in Teacher Education." *Journal of Teacher Education,* 1996, *47,* 253–262.

Charney, D., and Carlson, R. A. "Learning to Write in a Genre: What Student Writers Take from Model Texts." *Research in the Teaching of English,* 1995, *29,* 88–125.

Claggett, F. *A Measure of Success.* Portsmouth, N.H.: Boynton/Cook, 1996.

Cochran-Smith, M., and Lytle, S. *Inside/Outside: Teacher Research and Knowledge.* New York: Teachers College Press, 1993.

Daiker, D., and Morenberg, M. (eds.). *The Writing Teacher as Researcher.* Portsmouth, N.H.: Boynton/Cook, 1990.

Davies, A., Cameron, C., Politano, C., and Gregory, K. *Together is Better: Collaborative Assessment, Evaluation, and Reporting.* Winnipeg, Manitoba: Peguis, 1992.

Dysthe, O. "The Multivoiced Classroom: Interactions of Writing and Classroom Discourse." *Written Communication,* 1996, *13,* 383–425.

Elbow, P., and Belanoff, P. "State University of New York at Stony Brook Portfolio-Based Evaluation Program." In P. Belanoff and M. Dickson (eds.), *Portfolios: Process and Product* Portsmouth, N.H.: Boynton/Cook, 1991.

Herrington, A., and Curtin, M. "Basic Writing: Moving the Voices on the Margin to the Center." *Harvard Educational Review,* 1990, *60,* 489–496.

Hughes, D., and Keeling, B. "The Use of Model Essays to Reduce Context Effects in Essay Scoring." *Journal of Educational Measurement,* 1984, *21,* 277–281.

Jolliffe, D. A. "Audience, Subject, Form, and Ways of Speaking: Writers' Knowledge in the Disciplines." *Dissertation Abstracts International,* 1985, *46,* 367A.

Mathison, M. A. "Writing the Critiques: A Text About a Text." *Written Communication,* 1996, *13,* 314–354.

Macrorie, K. *The I-Search Paper: Revised Edition of Searching Writing.* Portsmouth, N.H.: Boynton/Cook, 1988.

Mishler, E. "Validation in Inquiry-Guided Research: The Role of Exemplars in Narrative Studies." *Harvard Educational Review,* 1990, *60,* 415–422.

Murray, D. "Internal Revision: A Process of Discovery." In C. Cooper and L. Odell (eds.), *Research on Composing: Points of Departure.* Urbana, Ill.: National Council of Teachers of English, 1978.

Newkirk, T. "How Students Read Student Papers: An Exploratory Study." *Written Communication,* 1984, *1,* 283–305.

Rose, M. *Lives on the Boundary.* New York: Pilgrim, 1989.

Schon, D. A. *Educating the Reflective Practitioner: Toward a New Design for Teaching and Learning in the Professions.* San Francisco: Jossey-Bass, 1987.

Short, K., and Burke, C. *Creating Curriculum: Teachers and Students as a Community of Learners.* Portsmouth, N.H.: Heinemann, 1991.

Smagorinsky, P. "Appropriating Tools for Teaching and Research Through Collaborative Independent Study." *English Education,* 1996, *28,* 127–142.

Stiggins, R. J. *Student-Centered Classroom Assessment.* (2nd ed.) New York: Merrill, 1997.

Sweedler-Brown, C. "The Influence of Training and Experience on Holistic Essay Evaluations." *English Journal,* 1985, *74,* 49–55.

Westerhoff, H. J. "The Teacher as a Pilgrim." In F. S. Bolin and J. M. Falk (eds.), *Teacher Renewal.* New York: Teachers College Press, 1987.

Wilkinson, L., and Silliman, E. "Alternative Assessment, Literacy Education, and School Reform." In J. Flood, S. B. Heath, D. Lapp (eds.), *Handbook on Research on Teaching Literacy Through Communicative and Visual Arts.* New York: Macmillan, 1997.

Zinsser, W. *Writing to Learn.* New York: Harper and Row, 1988.

Zinsser, W. *On Writing Well.* (4th ed.) New York: HarperCollins, 1990.

BEVERLY BUSCHING is professor of education at the University of South Carolina and director of the Midlands Writing Project.

Professional programs have discovered the importance of moving their students into "real-world" settings for professional preparation. This chapter offers a field-based evaluation framework that is longitudinal, contextualized, and collaborative. Portfolios are offered as one tool that fits this framework.

Grading Student Performance in Real-World Settings

Patricia A. Scanlon, Michael P. Ford

As professors learn more about situated learning (Anderson, Reder, and Simon, 1996) and the importance of context in learning experiences (Rhodes and Dudley-Marling, 1996), they begin to see the need to reconceptualize professional preparation programs. Reaching beyond the walls of traditional classroom settings, educators in a wide variety of professional programs have discovered the importance of moving their students into "real-world" settings for professional preparation (Darling-Hammond, 1990; Gibson, 1996). This trend is reflected in the current interest in movements such as school-to-work projects in education (Hartoonian and Van Scotter, 1996) and field-based professional internships in health care (Stern and Rahn, 1995). In our field, teacher education, we have seen an increase in the collaboration between universities and local school districts (Wilmore, 1996). Other fields have also seen the walls between the classroom and the world of work begin to disappear.

When students integrate the world of work with their course work, it impacts how professors teach, what professors teach, and how student learning is evaluated (Toohey, Ryan, and Hughes, 1996). It is the latter issue we focus on in this chapter. What happens to traditional evaluation techniques when students' course work includes practical work in world-of-work contexts?

Emerging Questions from Our Professional Field

Our responsibility is the preparation of elementary school teachers. We share the view with professors in programs such as business, nursing, and social work that course work that includes practical or field experiences in "real-work" settings enables candidates to integrate their understandings of theory and practice into their professional knowledge base. Practical experiences also enable students to develop more professional attitudes and strengthen their self-esteem.

Our experience has supported our belief in the value of integrating field experiences and professional course work. Our college developed an integrated block of professional methods courses with a strong field component. Undergraduate students no longer took separate methods courses removed from K–12 classrooms, but instead formed a learning community in which they took integrated courses connected to the field. This learning community brought together College of Education faculty, classroom teacher mentors, and university students to discuss how preparations for learning about teaching might be best accomplished.

This learning community concept caused us to re-examine our approaches to teaching and evaluation. One challenge became how to grade the connections students made between their university course work and their experiences in the field. How could we support students' thoughtful connections between classroom theories and practical work? It became apparent to us that traditional assessment measures (such as tests and quizzes) did not capture the scope of students' learning and growth. We concluded that alternative forms of evaluation were necessary to more adequately represent students' growth and change (Ohlhausen and Ford, 1992).

A Framework for Thinking About Evaluation of Practical Experience

Although we have long recognized the dilemma of evaluation and grading in our own professional lives, research suggests that the challenge of grading is age-long (Milton, Pollio, and Eison, 1986; Guskey, 1994). In fact, Newman (1992) identifies three somewhat conflicting purposes for evaluation. This multipurpose nature of evaluation is in part what makes it so difficult to assign one grade to student learning.

Grading student work becomes even more complicated when students are involved in diverse professional settings that provide a variety of valuable professional experiences. According to Guskey (1994), any system constructed for evaluating and grading students must do two things: (1) provide accurate and understandable descriptions of learning; and (2) use grading and reporting methods to enhance, not hinder, teaching and learning. Data to assess students' practical work should be collected in a variety of ways and from a variety of sources, including evaluation forms, student logs or journals, observations by field and university supervisors, self-evaluations, and samples of professional work. Patterns of student performance representing the professional development of students will emerge as these data are examined and analyzed (Wiggins, 1993). Evaluation of students in professional settings should be longitudinal, contextual, and collaborative (Sorenson, 1992).

Evaluation Should Be Longitudinal.   Professional growth and development is an individual process that occurs over an extended period of time and requires longitudinal collection of evaluation information. For example, the knowledge, skills, and dispositions of a student in a family nurse practitioner program can be expected to change and improve with experience (Barker, 1997). This may be evident through the use of a clinical log kept by the student, through observations made by the on-site or university supervisor, or through the use of mid-term and final evaluation forms completed by both the field supervisor and the student that list family nurse practitioner skills the student is developing. In teacher education, we expect a student teacher to focus on improving the individual needs of students as he or she works in a particular classroom setting. In social work, the intern is expected to improve his or her knowledge of an agency's policies and procedures over time. Further, the intern's skills and confidence in working with a particular client should also increase. Evaluation of students in any of these settings is most beneficial when the longitudinal nature of learning is acknowledged.

Evaluation Should Be Contextualized.   It makes no sense to assess students' practical work unless the situation in which they did the work is used to inform the assessment. This means that students are held accountable for the quality of the work that was performed in a particular situation. Evaluation can be contextualized by observations made in the professional setting, as well as with work samples documenting work performed in that setting. Samples may include such artifacts as a public relations brochure developed for a particular client or the final market report analyzing financial data in a particular business context. These brochures and reports would be evaluated for their clarity, comprehensiveness, and value to the company. Work samples that "count" as data for evaluation in any work setting should always be considered with the professional context in mind. Contextual limitations, support systems, and "rules" of operation, as well as interns' efforts and abilities, will undoubtedly influence students' products, performances, and professional growth.

Evaluation Should Be Collaborative.   Collaborative evaluation suggests that all parties involved in students' professional growth—the university supervisor, the field agency supervisor, and the students—should be involved in the evaluation process. Students' involvement is crucial because self-evaluation, as well as feedback from other informed professionals, provides the basis for developing skills that the student can use to become a lifelong learner. In a business internship or an internship in a legal setting, the student and the field supervisor might each complete a mid-term evaluation form. Using this common form provides a basis for discussing the student's strengths and some areas where further growth is needed. In a system where student self-evaluation is valued, the intern would be invited to share his or her evaluation first, thus supporting the development of self-reflection, a skill that cannot be developed when only external feedback is provided. In either of these settings, the ability to use work samples as evidence of the student's growth and learning would also provide valuable experience in self-evaluation.

Learning from Experience: The Challenges of Evaluating Practical Work

There are clearly strengths in providing students with practical work experiences as part of their professional preparation. Two areas that are especially challenging are the context in which the experience occurs and the ability to promote lifelong professional learning.

Being Sensitive to Context.   Placing students in work environments does not guarantee that those environments will provide the same learning opportunities for all students. In the case of a public relations (PR) internship, for example, students may be assigned to positions in highly different settings, depending on their area of interest. The intern's PR position may be with a corporation, a nonprofit agency, a small or large hospital, or a major league sports team. In each of these settings, the kinds of work the students do will vary greatly. Therefore, the ways assessment data are collected must be broad enough to capture evidence of the students' knowledge and skills in a variety of situations. The evaluation instruments, however, must also be specific enough to provide the student, the mentor, and the instructor with common expectations for the learning that occurs in this setting. Likewise, the process used for grading must be sensitive to the diversity of these experiences without penalizing or rewarding students on the basis of the experiences available to them in their professional contexts.

One possible solution for addressing this concern is to engage all three stakeholders in extensive conversations about expectations, experiences, and evaluation. One example for creating this dialogue is a student learning contract developed by the Social Work Department at our university (Ward, 1997). This contract is constructed during the first five weeks of the field experience and requires the instructor and students to identify field-site activities the students will perform to meet program goals related to accreditation. This contract is initially signed by students, the instructor, and the agency supervisor. Progress is monitored through weekly student-supervisor conferences, a mid-term review with the instructor, and a final three-way conference.

Promoting Lifelong Professional Learning.   In many professions, supervision of one's work occurs relatively infrequently. Although biannual reviews and observations may occur in some professional settings, external feedback is minimal (Brandt, 1996). Improvement and growth as professionals requires daily reflection and self-evaluation; it also requires the individual to problem solve and to initiate change to make improvements where they seem necessary. Professionals need to be able to look at their work, critically analyze what they are doing, and make changes as needed to strengthen their practices.

Unfortunately, many university students have spent numerous years in professional programs in which the evaluation of their work constantly involved external feedback. Students have been given relatively few opportunities to direct, document, and evaluate their own learning. Without these experiences and skills, approaching one's professional work as a lifelong learner is unlikely.

The process for grading students' practical work should foster habits of reflection and self-evaluation to promote ways of thinking about professional work that supports individual change and improvement. We have discovered the value of a learning portfolio as a tool for promoting reflection and self-evaluation as students work to direct and document their own learning.

Portfolio Development

For us, the portfolio has become a powerful tool that addresses the longitudinal, contextual, and collaborative nature of assessment. We begin the process by negotiating with students the identification of outcomes. We ask them, "What should students know and be able to do at the end of this experience?" Students often suggest increased ability to plan lessons, apply ideas gained from class in practical settings, and build their own personal levels of confidence, competence, and comfort in the role of teacher. Outcomes such as these provide a natural bridge between university course work and field experience.

A discussion is held to identify what types of evidence might be used to document growth and change toward these outcomes. Students begin to realize that samples and examples of their field experience work might be the best evidence for showing their ability to apply ideas and concepts explored in their course work.

Finally, students are involved in creating criteria for judging the evidence and the successful completion of the outcomes. (See Exhibits 10.1 and 10.2 for sample criteria.) These criteria are intentionally broad to encompass a variety of ways of documenting students' learning, but they provide a specific framework so that they could used by professors, teacher mentors, and university students in the evaluation process (Ford, Anderson, Bruneau, and Scanlan, 1996).

Once issues about outcomes, evidence, and criteria have been decided, students are invited to begin the portfolio process. Time is set aside throughout the semester during the university class for students to share their developing portfolios with one another. This type of peer interaction is critical for encouraging students to learn from one another's work experiences. Since students are documenting events in different professional settings, the sharing of portfolios allows students to drop in on other teaching situations (Ohlhausen and Ford, 1992).

Throughout the semester, as students select evidence that documents their learning, they also are asked to reflect on evidence included in their portfolios. Students are asked to use captions (Evans and Vavrus, 1990) to explain what a piece of evidence is, what context it comes from, why it is important enough to be included in the portfolio, how it indicates growth and change, and how it shows connections between their work experience and class content. In these captions, students can further explain how their understandings changed because of their field experience, what they are learning on the job, and what struggles they are encountering.

Exhibit 10.1. Suggested Rubric for Portfolios

1. Quantity of Items:

None   Appropriate number of comparable pieces

◄──►

2. Creativity (for example, creative application of ideas, went beyond class requirements, sought out unfamiliar information)

Creativity lacking   Highly creative

◄──►

3. Level of Reflection

Minimal reflection   Significant reflection throughout

◄──►

4. Appropriateness of Evidence (for example, evidence supports narrative, fits purpose, is relevant for goal)

Appropriateness lacking   Appropriateness evident

◄──►

5. Usefulness of Ideas to Future Teaching and Learning Contexts

Little potential for future use   Significant potential for future use

◄──►

6. Self-Initiated Section

Not included   Well developed

◄──►

7. Quality of Change

Little evidence of change   Significant change documented

◄──►

8. Variety of Activities and Evidence

Very narrow range   Wide range

◄──►

9. Organization

Unclear organization   Very viewer friendly

◄──►

10. Time and Effort Invested

Little evidence of time and effort   Significant evidence of time and effort

◄──►

Exhibit 10.2. Criteria for Portfolio Evaluation

Portfolio Content

1. Portfolio includes evidence of learning and related reflections about the teaching of reading and about my growth as a teacher of reading.

| Little evidence of learning, change, and growth | Some evidence of learning, change, and growth | Lots of evidence of learning, change, and growth |

Comments:

2. Portfolio includes evidence of developing understandings about and/or applications of course concepts.

| Little evidence | Some evidence | Lots of evidence |

Comments:

3. Portfolio includes typed reflections on learning, growth, and change which include specific examples, explanations, and a sense of personal involvement in the learning process.

| Little specificity, explanation and sense of personal involvement | Some specificity, explanation and sense of personal involvement | Lots of specificity, explanation and sense of personal involvement |

Comments:

Portfolio Form

4. Portfolio is presented in a manner that is well-organized, understandable, and well-edited.

| Little attention to presentation | Some attention to presentation | Lots of attention to presentation |

Comments:

5. Portfolio shows evidence of effort.

| Little evidence of effort | Some evidence of effort | Lots of evidence of effort |

Comments:

The end of the semester necessitates closure on the portfolio experience. It also requires the assignment of grades. We have experimented with a variety of approaches in grading portfolios (Ford, Anderson, Bruneau, and Scanlan, 1996). Using a student-centered approach, one strategy was to invite the students to self-evaluate and grade their portfolios according to negotiated criteria. The instructor reviewed those decisions and conferred with each student to reach consensus about a final grade (Ford, 1996). In a more teacher-directed approach, the instructor can retain full control of the grading decision by using criteria outlined for students (Stahle and Mitchell, 1993). When it has been possible to coordinate with professors in other learning community courses, portfolios have sometimes been read and graded independently by two professors who later conferred with the student to determine a final portfolio grade. An external reviewer from the field who is knowledgeable about the university's professional program might also be invited to participate in evaluating the students' portfolios (Scanlan and Heiden, 1996).

Conclusion

Evaluation that is longitudinal, contextualized, and collaborative will provide professional programs with assessment information about students' professional development. When evaluating the practical work of students, professors should use a variety of sources for assessment data. Despite a framework that uses alternative assessments, the assignment of grades still requires a professional judgment on the part of university faculty. There is no way to systematize the task of assigning grades to perfectly assess student learning. Using a variety of sources of information that is collected over time in the professional context by the field agency supervisor, the instructor and the student ensure a more informed professional judgment than traditional tests and score sheets can produce. In the complex world required of professionals today, there are no precise systems for determining single grades to describe student learning. Professional sense, clear thinking, careful planning, excellent communication skills, and overriding concern for students are still required.

References

Anderson, J. R., Reder, L. M., and Simon, H. "Situated Learning and Education." *Educational Researcher,* 1996, 25, 5–11.

Barker, M. *College of Nursing Documents.* Oshkosh: University of Wisconsin, Oshkosh, 1997.

Brandt, R. "On a New Direction for Teacher Evaluation: A Conversation with Tom McGreal." *Educational Leadership,* 1996, 53, 30–33.

Darling-Hammond, L. *The Teaching Internship: Practical Preparation for a Licensed Profession.* Santa Monica, Calif.: The Rand Corporation, 1990.

Evans, K. S., and Vavrus, L. G. "The Role of Document Captions in Student Portfolios as a Link Between Teacher and Student Assessment." Paper presented at the annual meeting of the National Reading Conference, Miami Beach, Fla., December 1990.

Ford, M. P. "Begin with the End in Sight: Student Negotiated Evaluation in a Preservice Literacy Education Course." *New Era in Education Journal,* 1996, 77 (1), 2–8.

Ford, M. P., Anderson, R., Bruneau, B., and Scanlan, P. "Student Portfolios in Four Literacy Education Contexts: Challenging Decisions About Evaluation and Grading." In D. Leu, C. Kinzer, and K. Hinchman (eds.), *Literacies for the 21st Century: Research and Practice—Forty-Fifth Yearbook of the National Reading Conference Yearbook.* Chicago, Ill.: National Reading Conference, 1996.

Gibson, D. "Criteria for Establishing and Evaluating Public Relations Internship Systems." *Public Relations Quarterly,* 1996, 41, 43–45.

Guskey, T. "Making the Grade: What Benefits Students? *Educational Leadership,* 1994, 52 (2), 14–20.

Hartoonian, M., and Van Scotter, R. "School-to-Work: A Model for Learning a Living." *Phi Delta Kappan,* 1996, 77, 555–560.

Milton, O., Pollio, H., and Eison, J. *Making Sense of College Grades*. San Francisco: Jossey-Bass, 1986.

Newman, J. "Yes, But What About Evaluation?" In K. Goodman (ed.), *The Whole Language Catalog Supplement on Authentic Assessment*. Santa Rosa, Calif.: Macmillan-McGraw Hill, 1992.

Ohlhausen, M., and Ford, M. "The Promise and Process of Portfolio Assessment in Literacy Education Classes." In A. Frager and J. Miller (eds.), *Using Inquiry in Reading Education*. Canton, Ohio: The College Reading Association, 1992.

Rhodes, L. K., and Dudley-Marling, C. *Readers and Writers with a Difference: A Holistic Approach to Teaching Struggling Readers and Writers* (2nd ed.). Portsmouth, N.H.: Heinemann, 1996.

Scanlan, P. A., and Heiden, D. E. "External Review of Portfolios in Preservice Teacher Education: Studying Our Own Practice." *Reading Horizons*, 1996, *36*, 297–316.

Sorenson, N. "Making Evaluation Longitudinal: Evaluation as History Writing." In K. Goodman (ed.), *The Whole Language Catalog Supplement on Authentic Assessment*. Santa Rosa, Calif.: Macmillan-McGraw Hill, 1992.

Stahle, D. L., and Mitchell, J. "Portfolio Assessment in College Methods Courses: Practicing What We Preach." *The Journal of Reading*, 1993, *36*, 538–542.

Stern, D., and Rahn, M. "How Health Career Academies Provide Work-Based Learning." *Educational Leadership*, 1995, *52*, 37–40.

Toohey, S., Ryan, G., and Hughes, C. "Assessing the Practicum." *Assessment and Evaluation in Higher Education*, 1996, *21* (3), 215–228.

Ward, J. *Social Work Department Documents*, Oshkosh, Wis.: University of Wisconsin, Oshkosh, 1997.

Wiggins, G. "Assessment: Authenticity, Context, and Validity. *Phi Delta Kappan*, 1993, *75* (3), 200–214.

Wilmore, E. "Brave New World: Field-Based Teacher Preparation." *Educational Leadership*, 1996, *53*, 59–63.

PATRICIA A. SCANLON is associate professor in the Reading Education Department at the University of Wisconsin, Oshkosh, where she teaches both graduate and undergraduate courses.

MICHAEL P. FORD is associate professor in the Reading Education Department at the University of Wisconsin, Oshkosh, where he teaches both graduate and undergraduate courses.

INDEX

Academic standards: and assessment, 23–26

Adams, D. M., 82, 85

Agnew, E., 23

Allen, I., 27

Alternative assessment: philosophy and theory of, 9, 10–11; shift to, 5–13; versus traditional assessment, 7–11. *See also* Constructivism

Anderson, D. S., 7

Anderson, J. R., 97

Anderson, R. S., 3, 101, 103

Andrew, M., 92–93

Angelo, T. A., 28, 38

Archbald, D. A., 10

Armato, C., 79

Asbacher, P. R., 8, 10

Assessment: and academic standards, 23–26; constructivist paradigm for, 11–13; of cooperative group projects, 63–64; ethical issues in, 26–28; formative versus summative, 12, 22–23; key components of, 65; of portfolios, 82–84; rubric-guided, 92–95; shift from traditional to alternative, 5–13; of technology-based products, 69–77. *See also* Evaluation; Grading

Astin, A. W., 60

Ballard, L., 80, 82, 84

Barbour, D. H., 26

Barker, M., 99

Baron, J. B., 35

Barrows, H. S., 69

Bean, J. C., 3, 38

Becker, H. S., 66

Belanger, J., 26

Belanoff, P., 5, 18, 24, 93

Belcher, D. D., 27

Bell, S., 79

Berlak, H., 8

Berrisford, T., 17

Bertrand, J. E., 8

Bhide, A., 38

Bintz, W. P., 6, 7, 10, 11

Bishop, W., 95

Black, L., 85

Block, M. N., 5, 6

Bloom, B. S., 34, 37, 39

Bonwell, C. C., 51

Boud, D., 27

Brandt, R., 100

Branthwaite, A., 17

Brooks, J. G., 7

Brooks, M. G., 7

Brown, B. J., 24, 80

Brown, R., 80

Bruffee, K. A., 34

Bruneau, B., 101, 103

Bruner, J., 7

Bryant, L., 24, 79, 80

Bryde, S., 7

Bufkin, L. J., 7

Bullock, R., 25

Burke, C., 6, 10, 11, 93

Burton, J. K., 27

Busching, B., 4

Calfee, R. C., 22, 85

Cameron, C., 93

Campbell, J. A., 41, 45

Carlson, R. A., 93

Carlson, R. E., 43

Carr, K. S., 7

Carroll, J. A., 93

Charney, D., 93

Chase, C. I., 33

Claggett, F. A., 94

Clark, B. L., 28

Classroom participation: alternative assessment of, 36–38; grading of, 33–39; modes of, 34; problem areas in, 38–39; rubric for, 36

Cochran-Smith, M., 91

Cognition and Technology Group at Vanderbilt, 69

Cohen, A. D., 28

Cohen, A. S., 24

Cold-calling format, 34

Condon, W., 24

Constructivism: assessment paradigm based on, 11–13; and instructional technology, 69–70; and language of grading, 21–22; and need for alternative assessment, 7

Cooper, W., 24, 80

Cooperative projects, 59–66
Cronin, M. W., 41, 42
Crooks, T. J., 5
Cross, K. P., 38
Curtin, M., 93
Curtis, D. B., 7

Daiker, D. A., 26, 27, 91–92
Darling-Hammond, L., 97
Davies, A., 92–93
Davis, B. G., 33, 39
Davydov, V. V., 7
Deane, D., 27
Deming, M. P., 79, 80, 82
Deutsch, M., 66
Dickson, M., 5
Diedrich, P. B., 17
Dixon-Krauss, L., 7
Dohrer, G., 28
Donovan, S., 66
Dowling, N. M., 24
Dragga, S., 27
Ducheine, M., 79
Duckworth, E., 7
Dudley-Marling, C., 97
Duffy, T. M., 69
Dulek, R., 17
Dykstra, D. I., Jr., 12–13
Dysthe, O., 93

Eddy, D. M., 17
Ede, L., 26
Edwards, D., 17
Eison, J. A., 33, 51, 60, 98
Elbow, P., 93
Email, and class participation, 38. See also
   Listserve discussions
Emig, J., 51
Engel, B. S., 8
Evaluation: formative and summative, 12;
   of instructional technology, 69–77; of
   portfolios, 101–104; of practical expe-
   rience, 98–10. See also Assessment;
   Grading
Evans, K. S., 101
Evans, S., 19

Farr, B. P., 6
Fisher, A., 37–38
Fishman, B., 69
Fiske, D. W., 17
Flach, J., 5, 21

Flaum, D., 41
Fogg, L., 17
Ford, M. P., 4, 80, 98, 101, 103
Formative assessment, 12, 22–23: for
   cooperative projects, 61–63
Fosnot, C. W., 7
Frazier, D., 79
Freedman, S. W., 22
Freire, P., 8
Freisem, K., 46

Gale, J., 7
Gay, P., 79
Geer, B., 66
Gibson, D., 97
Glasson, G. E., 6
Glenn, P., 41
Gomez, M. L., 5, 6
Gottlieb, M., 24
Grading: of classroom participation,
   33–39; of cooperative projects, 59–66;
   criterion-versus   norm-referenced,
   60–61; of inquiry projects, 89–95; lan-
   guage of, 19–23; of oral assignments,
   41–48; positivist versus constructivist
   approach to, 21–22; and professional
   judgment, 17–29; in real-world set-
   tings, 97–104; of written assignments,
   51–57. See also Assessment; Evaluation
Grady, E., 69
Graue, M. E., 5, 6
Greenbaum, S., 27
Greenberg, J. B., 7
Greene, M., 10
Gregory, K., 92–93
Grice, G. L., 42
Grogan, N., 26
Gruender, C. D., 7
Guskey, T., 98

Halpern, D., 6
Hamm, M. E., 82, 85
Hamp-Lyons, L., 24
Hannafin, M. J., 69
Harris, J., 21
Harris, M., 28
Harste, J., 10
Hartoonian, M., 97
Hassencahl, F., 27
Heffernan, J.A.W., 27
Heiden, D. E., 104
Helton, E., 85

Hendrix, K. G., 46
Heron, J., 8, 11
Herman, D., 8, 10
Herrington, A., 93
Hillocks, G., Jr., 19, 21
Hobson, E. H., 3, 51
Holder, C., 64
Honebein, P., 69
Hopper, R., 41
Huber, T., 93
Hughes, C., 97
Hughes, D., 93
Hughes, E. C., 66
Hull, G. A., 28
Humphreys, W. L., 18
Hutchings, P., 10
Hysmith, C., 79

Inquiry projects, 89–95
Instructors: and academic freedom, 24–25; as coach and judge, 26; insufficient training of, 25–26; professional judgment of, 17–29
Internet, 69–77
I-Search Paper, The, 93

Jackson, D. S., 23
Jacobs, L. C., 33
Janzow, F., 33
Johnson, D. W., 34, 60, 64, 65, 66
Johnson, F. P., 34
Johnson, R. T., 60, 64, 65, 66
Johnston, P. H., 10, 11
Jolliffe, D. A., 94
Jonassen, D. J., 69, 70
Jones, T., 26

Kane, M. B., 5
Karnes, M. R., 6
Keeling, B., 93
Kline, C. R., Jr., 19
Knapp, J. V., 27
Knight, P., 24, 84
Kroll, B. M., 27
Kroll, L. R., 7

LaBoskey, V. K., 7
Lalik, R. V., 6
Lamme, L. L., 79
Land, R. E., Jr., 19
Land, S. M., 69
Larson, R., 79

Learning: in alternative assessment, 10–11; and instructional technology, 69–77; versus performance, 1; in traditional assessment, 8, 10
Lecture: overuse of, 6
Listserv discussions, 70–72, 73
Lucas, S. E., 42
Lytle, S., 91

Macrorie, K., 90, 91–92, 93
MacGregor, T., 27
Manus, A. L., 12
Marino, R. P., 5
Marking, 19
Marzano, R., 33
Mathison, M. A., 94
McCulloch, J., 17
McDonald, W. U., Jr., 23
McKeachie, W. J., 6, 39
McLaughlin, M., 5
McNamara, M. J., 27
McTighe, J., 5
Meacham, J., 38
Metzger, E., 24, 79, 80
Meyer, C., 79
Michaels, W., 6
Mishler, E., 89
Milton, O., 60, 98
Mitchell, J., 80, 85, 103
Mitchell, R., 5
Mittan, R., 27
Modaff, J., 41
Moll, L. C., 7
Morenberg, M., 91–92
Morreale, S., 42
Morrison, G. R., 3, 69
Moss, A., 64
Mullin, J. A., 4
Murphy, J. M., 46
Murphy, S., 22, 79
Murray, D., 93–94

Nelson, P. E., 42
Newkirk, N., 28, 93
Newman, F. M., 10
Newman, J., 98
Nuhfer, E. B., 62
Nyquist, J. D., 46
Nystrand, M., 24

Objective tests: overuse of, 6
Odle, C., 7

Ohlhausen, M., 98, 101
Olson, J., 79, 80, 82
On Writing Well, 93
Oral assignments: design of, 42–43; grading criteria, 43–48; rationale for, 41–42
Osborn, M., 42, 43
Osborn, S., 42, 43

Palmer, P., 79
Paulson, F. L., 79
Paulson, P., 79
Pearson, J. C., 42
Performance: versus learning, 1; in real-world settings, 97–104
Perfumo, P., 85
Perrone, V., 5–6
Peterson, D. 3, 36–37, 38
Piaget, J., 7
Piazza, J. A., 7
Pickering, P., 5
Politano, C., 92–93
Pollio, H. R., 18, 60, 98
Portfolios: and academic standards, 24; advantages and challenges of, 85–86; assessment of, 82–84; benefits of, 79–82; development of, 101–104; future of, 86
Positivism: assessment based on, 5–10; and language of grading, 21
Potthoff, D., 93
Professional judgment, 17–29
Professors. See Instructors

Quellmalz, E., 37
Quigley, B. L., 3, 46

Rahn, M., 97
Raven, J., 8, 10
Reder, L. M., 97
Reed, W. M., 27
Rhodes, L. K., 97
Robinson II, T. E., 46
Roderick, J. A., 10
Rose, M., 93
Ross, C., 17
Ross, S. M., 3, 69
Rubel, E., 37
Russell, D. R., 51
Ryan, G., 97

Sager, C., 66
Sanders, N. M., 37
Savery, J. R., 69

Sawyer, T. M., 26
Scanlon, P. A., 4, 101, 103, 104
Schafer, J. C., 27
Schafermeyer, K. W., 51
Schon, D. A., 89
Sessions, R., 8
Shelby, A., 17
Shepard, L. A., 5
Shockley-Zalabak, P., 42
Short, K. G., 6, 10, 11, 93
Shulman, L. S., 5
Silliman, E., 92–93
Simon, H., 97
Sloan, G., 25
Smagorinsky, P., 89
Smith, E., 28
Smith, K. A., 3, 60, 66
Smith-Howell, D., 43
Sommers, J., 85
Sorenson, N., 98
Speck, B. W., 3, 26, 27
Spicuzza, F., 81, 82
Sprague, J., 43
Springer, L., 66
Stahle, D., 80, 85, 103
Stanne, M. E., 66
Steffe, L. P., 7
Steinfatt, T., 41
Stern, D., 97
Sternberg, R. J., 6
Stiggins, R. J., 37, 92–93
Stuart, D., 43
Students: classroom participation of, 33–39; in cooperative group projects, 62; development of rubrics by, 12–13, 54–56; diversity of, 6; evaluation of, 13; self-assessment of, 80–81; self-esteem of, 82
Summative assessment, 12, 22–23
Sweedler-Brown, C., 93

Taylor, C. T., 70
Taylor, J., 27
Technology-based learning, 69–77
Tellez, K., 5
Tittle, C. K., 7
Toohey, S., 97
Total Quality Management (TQM), 62
Traditional assessment: versus alternative assessment, 7–11; philosophy and theory of, 7–10; shift away from, 5–13. See *also* Positivism
Tritt, M., 26

Trueman, M., 17
Trumbull, E., 6

Valencia, S. W., 24
Valeri-Gold, M., 79, 80, 82
Van Scotter, R., 97
Vavrus, L. G., 101
Vogt, M., 5–6
Vygotsky, L. S., 7

Wall, S. V., 28
Waller, A. A., 60
Ward, J., 100
Weeks, F. W., 23
Westerhoff, H. J., 89
White, E. M., 24, 34, 52, 54
Whitney, P., 42

Wiggins, G., 5, 80, 98
Wilkinson, L., 92–93
Williams, J. M., 27
Wilmore, E., 97
Wilson, S. M., 5
Winsor, J. L., 7
Winters, L., 8, 10
Witte, S. P., 5, 21
Wolf, D. P., 10, 79, 80
Written assignments: design of, 52–54; grading rubric for, 56; and inquiry projects, 89–95; rationale for, 51–52; student-based assessment of, 54–56
Writing to Learn, 93

Zak, F., 27
Zinsser, W., 93

Ordering Information

NEW DIRECTIONS FOR TEACHING AND LEARNING is a series of paperback books that presents ideas and techniques for improving college teaching, based both on the practical expertise of seasoned instructors and on the latest research findings of educational and psychological researchers. Books in the series are published quarterly in Spring, Summer, Fall, and Winter and are available for purchase by subscription as well as by single copy.

SUBSCRIPTIONS cost $54.00 for individuals (a savings of 35 percent over single-copy prices) and $90.00 for institutions, agencies, and libraries. Please do not send institutional checks for personal subscriptions. Standing orders are accepted. Prices subject to change. (For subscriptions outside of North America, add $7.00 for shipping via surface mail or $25.00 for air mail. Orders must be prepaid in U.S. dollars by check drawn on a U.S. bank or charged to VISA, MasterCard, or American Express.)

SINGLE COPIES cost $22.00 plus shipping (see below) when payment accompanies order. California, New Jersey, New York, and Washington, D.C., residents please include appropriate sales tax. Canadian residents add GST and any local taxes. Billed orders will be charged shipping and handling. No billed shipments to post office boxes. (Orders from outside North America must be prepaid in U.S. dollars by check drawn on a U.S. bank or charged to VISA, MasterCard, or American Express.)

SHIPPING (SINGLE COPIES ONLY): $30.00 and under, add $5.50; to $50.00, add $6.50; to $75.00, add $7.50; to $100.00, add $9.00; to $150.00, add $10.00.

DISCOUNTS FOR QUANTITY ORDERS are available. Please write to the address below for information.

ALL ORDERS must include either the name of an individual or an official purchase order number. Please submit your order as follows:
Subscriptions: specify series and year subscription is to begin
Single copies: include individual title code (such as TL54)

MAIL ORDERS TO:
Jossey-Bass Publishers
350 Sansome Street
San Francisco, CA 94104-1342

PHONE subscription or single-copy orders toll-free at (888) 378-2537 or at (415) 433-1767 (toll call).

FAX orders toll-free to: (800) 605-2665

FOR SUBSCRIPTION SALES OUTSIDE OF THE UNITED STATES CONTACT:
any international subscription agency or Jossey-Bass directly.

OTHER TITLES AVAILABLE IN THE
NEW DIRECTIONS FOR TEACHING AND LEARNING SERIES
Robert J. Menges, Editor-in-Chief
Marilla D. Svinicki, Associate Editor

TL73 Academic Service Learning: A Pedagogy of Action and Reflection, *Robert A. Rhoads, Jeffrey P.F. Howard*
TL72 Universal Challenges in Faculty Work: Fresh Perspectives from Around the World, *Patricia Cranton*
TL71 Teaching and Learning at a Distance: What It Takes to Effectively Design, Deliver, and Evaluate Programs, *Thomas E. Cyrs*
TL70 Approaches to Teaching Non-Native English Speakers Across the Curriculum, *David L. Sigsbee, Bruce W. Speck, Bruce Maylath*
TL69 Writing to Learn: Strategies for Assigning and Responding to Writing Across the Disciplines, *Mary Deane Sorcenelli, Peter Elbow*
TL68 Bringing Problem-Based Learning to Higher Education: Theory and Practice, *LuAnn Wilkerson, Wim H. Gijselaers*
TL67 Using Active Learning in College Classes: A Range of Options for Faculty, *Tracey E. Sutherland, Charles C. Bonwell*
TL66 Ethical Dimensions of College and University Teaching: Understanding and Honoring the Special Relationship Between Teachers and Students, *Linc. Fisch*
TL65 Honoring Exemplary Teaching, *Marilla D. Svinicki, Robert J. Menges*
TL64 Disciplinary Differences in Teaching and Learning: Implications for Practice, *Nira Hativa, Michele Marincovich*
TL63 Understanding Self-Regulated Learning, *Paul R. Pintrich*
TL62 Teaching Through Academic Advising: A Faculty Perspective, *Alice G. Reinarz, Eric R. White*
TL61 Fostering Student Success in Quantitative Gateway Courses, *Joanne Gainen, Eleanor W. Willemsen*
TL60 Supplemental Instruction: Increasing Achievement and Retention, *Deanna C. Martin, David R. Arendale*
TL59 Collaborative Learning: Underlying Processes and Effective Techniques, *Kris Bosworth, Sharon J. Hamilton*
TL58 Interdisciplinary Studies Today, *Julie Thompson Klein, William G. Doty*
TL57 Mentoring Revisited: Making an Impact on Individuals and Institutions, *Marie A. Wunsch*
TL56 Student Self-Evaluation: Fostering Reflective Learning, *Jean MacGregor*
TL55 Developing Senior Faculty as Teachers, *Martin J. Finkelstein, Mark W. LaCelle-Peterson*
TL54 Preparing Faculty for the New Conceptions of Scholarship, *Laurie Richlin*
TL53 Building a Diverse Faculty, *Joanne Gainen, Robert Boice*
TL52 Promoting Diversity in College Classrooms: Innovative Responses for the Curriculum, Faculty, and Institutions, *Maurianne Adams*
TL51 Teaching in the Information Age: The Role of Educational Technology, *Michael J. Albright, David L. Graf*
TL50 Developing New and Junior Faculty, *Mary Deane Sorcinelli, Ann E. Austin*
TL49 Teaching for Diversity, *Laura L. B. Border, Nancy Van Note Chism*
TL48 Effective Practices for Improving Teaching, *Michael Theall, Jennifer Franklin*
TL47 Applying the Seven Principles for Good Practice in Undergraduate Education, *Arthur W. Chickering, Zelda F. Gamson*
TL46 Classroom Research: Early Lessons from Success, *Thomas A. Angelo*
TL45 College Teaching: From Theory to Practice, *Robert J. Menges, Marilla D. Svinicki*
TL44 Excellent Teaching in a Changing Academy: Essays in Honor of Kenneth Eble, *Feroza Jussawalla*

TL43   Student Ratings of Instruction: Issues for Improving Practice, *Michael Theall, Jennifer Franklin*

TL41   Learning Communities: Creating Connections Among Students, Faculty, and Disciplines, *Faith Gabelnick, Jean MacGregor, Roberta S. Matthews, Barbara Leigh Smith*

TL40   Integrating Liberal Learning and Professional Education, *Robert A. Armour, Barbara S. Fuhrmann*

TL39   Teaching Assistant Training in the 1990s, *Jody D. Nyquist, Robert D. Abbott*

TL38   Promoting Inquiry in Undergraduate Learning, *Frederick Stirton Weaver*

TL37   The Department Chairperson's Role in Enhancing College Teaching, *Ann F. Lucas*

TL36   Strengthening Programs for Writing Across the Curriculum, *Susan H. McLeod*

TL33   College Teaching and Learning: Preparing for New Commitments, *Robert E. Young, Kenneth E. Eble*

TL31   Techniques for Evaluating and Improving Instruction, *Lawrence M. Aleamoni*

TL30   Developing Critical Thinking and Problem-Solving Abilities, *James E. Stice*

TL29   Coping with Faculty Stress, *Peter Seldin*

TL28   Distinguished Teachers on Effective Teaching, *Peter G. Beidler*

TL26   Communicating in College Classrooms, *Jean M. Civikly*

TL21   Teaching as Though Students Mattered, *Joseph Katz*

TL14   Learning in Groups, *Clark Bouton, Russell Y. Garth*

TL12   Teaching Writing in All Disciplines, *C. Williams Griffin*

TL2   Learning, Cognition, and College Teaching, *Wilbert J. McKeachie*

Statement of Ownership, Management, and Circulation
(Required by 39 USC 3685)

1. Publication Title	2. Publication Number	3. Filing Date
NEW DIRECTIONS FOR TEACHING & LEARNING	0 2 7 1 - 0 6 3 3	9/15/97

4. Issue Frequency	5. Number of Issues Published Annually	6. Annual Subscription Price
QUARTERLY	4	$54 - indiv. $90 - instit.

7. Complete Mailing Address of Known Office of Publication (Not printer) (Street, city, county, state, and ZIP+4)	Contact Person
350 SANSOME STREET SAN FRANCISCO, CA 94104 (SAN FRANCISCO COUNTY)	ROGER HUNT Telephone 415 782 3232

8. Complete Mailing Address of Headquarters or General Business Office of Publisher (Not printer)

SAME AS ABOVE

9. Full Names and Complete Mailing Addresses of Publisher, Editor, and Managing Editor (Do not leave blank)
Publisher (Name and complete mailing address)

JOSSEY-BASS INC., PUBLISHERS
(ABOVE ADDRESS)

Editor (Name and complete mailing address) ROBERT J. MENGES
NORTHWESTERN UNIVERSITY
2115 NORTH CAMPUS DRIVE
EVANSTON, IL 60208-2610

Managing Editor (Name and complete mailing address)

NONE

10. Owner (Do not leave blank. If the publication is owned by a corporation, give the name and address of the corporation immediately followed by the names and addresses of all stockholders owning or holding 1 percent or more of the total amount of stock. If not owned by a corporation, give the names and addresses of the individual owners. If owned by a partnership or other unincorporated firm, give its name and address as well as those of each individual owner. If the publication is published by a nonprofit organization, give its name and address.)

Full Name	Complete Mailing Address
SIMON & SCHUSTER	P.O. BOX 1172
	ENGLEWOOD CLIFFS, NJ 07632-1172

11. Known Bondholders, Mortgagees, and Other Security Holders Owning or Holding 1 Percent or More of Total Amount of Bonds, Mortgages, or Other Securities. If none, check box. ▶ ☐ None

Full Name	Complete Mailing Address
SAME AS ABOVE	SAME AS ABOVE

12. Tax Status (For completion by nonprofit organizations authorized to mail at special rates) (Check one)
The purpose, function, and nonprofit status of this organization and the exempt status for federal income tax purposes:
☐ Has Not Changed During Preceding 12 Months
☐ Has Changed During Preceding 12 Months (Publisher must submit explanation of change with this statement)

PS Form 3526, September 1995   (See Instructions on Reverse)

---

13. Publication Title	14. Issue Date for Circulation Data Below
NEW DIRECTIONS FOR TEACHING & LEARNING	SUMMER 1997

15.	Extent and Nature of Circulation	Average No. Copies Each Issue During Preceding 12 Months	Actual No. Copies of Single Issue Published Nearest to Filing Date
a.	Total Number of Copies (Net press run)	1815	1973
b. Paid and/or Requested Circulation	(1) Sales Through Dealers and Carriers, Street Vendors, and Counter Sales (Not mailed)	340	104
	(2) Paid or Requested Mail Subscriptions (Include advertiser's proof copies and exchange copies)	782	813
c.	Total Paid and/or Requested Circulation (Sum of 15b(1) and 15b(2)) ▶	1122	917
d.	Free Distribution by Mail (Samples, complimentary, and other free)	0	0
e.	Free Distribution Outside the Mail (Carriers or other means)	157	203
f.	Total Free Distribution (Sum of 15d and 15e) ▶	157	203
g.	Total Distribution (Sum of 15c and 15f) ▶	1279	1120
h. Copies not Distributed	(1) Office Use, Leftovers, Spoiled	536	853
	(2) Returns from News Agents	0	0
i.	Total (Sum of 15g, 15h(1), and 15h(2)) ▶	1815	1973
	Percent Paid and/or Requested Circulation (15c / 15g x 100)	88%	82%

16. Publication of Statement of Ownership
☐ Publication required. Will be printed in the WINTER 1997 issue of this publication.
☐ Publication not required.

17. Signature and Title of Editor, Publisher, Business Manager, or Owner

SUSAN E. LEWIS,
DIRECTOR OF PERIODICALS   Date 9/18/97

I certify that all information furnished on this form is true and complete. I understand that anyone who furnishes false or misleading information on this form or who omits material or information requested on the form may be subject to criminal sanctions (including fines and imprisonment) and/or civil sanctions (including multiple damages and civil penalties).

Instructions to Publishers

1. Complete and file one copy of this form with your postmaster annually on or before October 1. Keep a copy of the completed form for your records.

2. In cases where the stockholder or security holder is a trustee, include in items 10 and 11 the name of the person or corporation for whom the trustee is acting. Also include the names and addresses of individuals who are stockholders who own or hold 1 percent or more of the total amount of bonds, mortgages, or other securities of the publishing corporation. In item 11, if none, check the box. Use blank sheets if more space is required.

3. Be sure to furnish all circulation information called for in item 15. Free circulation must be shown in items 15d, e, and f.

4. If the publication had second-class authorization as a general or requester publication, this Statement of Ownership, Management, and Circulation must be published; it must be printed in any issue in October or, if the publication is not published during October, the first issue printed after October.

5. In item 16, indicate the date of the issue in which this Statement of Ownership will be published.

6. Item 17 must be signed.

Failure to file or publish a statement of ownership may lead to suspension of second-class authorization.

PS Form 3526, September 1995 (Reverse)